Ireland Overview

- The Southwest
- The Southeast
- The North
- The West
- Dublin Walking Tour

0   20   40 KM

0   20   40 Mi.

1

Belfast

Sligo

Dublin

4

Limerick

Dingle

Youghal

3

2

D1373567

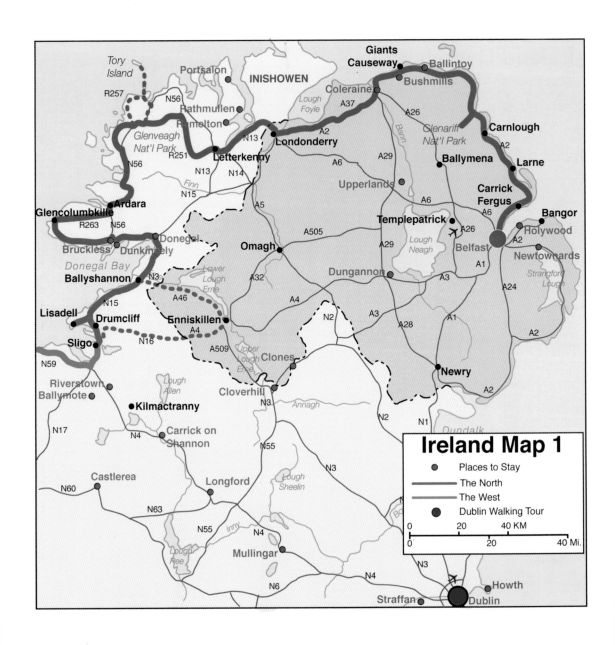

Tory Island
R257
N56
Portsalon
INISHOWEN
Giants Causeway
Ballintoy
Bushmills
Rathmullen
Ramelton
Coleraine
A37
Lough Foyle
A26
Glenariff Nat'l Park
Carnlough
Glenveagh Nat'l Park
N13
Londonderry
A2
Bann
Larne
A2
N56
R251
Letterkenny
Ballymena
N13
N14
A6
A29
Carrick Fergus
Finn
N15
A5
Upperlands
A6
Bangor
Ardara
Templepatrick
A26
Holywood
Glencolumbkille
R263 N56
Donegal
A505
A29
Lough Neagh
Belfast
Newtownards
Bruckless Dunkineely
Omagh
A1
Strangford Lough
Donegal Bay
N3
Lower Lough Erne
A32
Dungannon
A3
A24
Ballyshannon
A46
A4
A3
A1
A2
N15
Lisadell
Drumcliff
Enniskillen
A4
N2
A28
Sligo
N16
A509
Upper Lough Erne
Clones
Newry
N59
Riverstown
Lough Allen
Cloverhill
N3
Annagh
N2
A2
Ballymote
Kilmactranny
N1
Dundalk
N17
N4
Carrick on Shannon
N55
Castlerea
Longford
N3
N60
Lough Sheelin
N63
N55
Inny
N4
Lough Ree
Mullingar
N6
N4
N3
Howth
Straffan
Dublin

Ireland Map 1

● Places to Stay

— The North

— The West

● Dublin Walking Tour

0   20   40 KM
0   20   40 Mi.

Irish Sea

St. George's Channel

Ireland Map 2

- Places to Stay
- The Southwest
- The Southeast
- The West
- Dublin Walking Tour

0   20   40 KM
0   20   40 Mi.

N6
N4
Howth
Straffan
Dublin
N6
N62
N7
N52
N80
Naas
R115
Powerscourt
N65
Dunlavin
Ashford
Thor Balee
Terryglass
Portlaoise
Glendalough
Rathnew
Wicklow
N18
Lough Derg
N52
N7
R755
N11
Shannon
N9
Aughrim
R752
Abbeyleix
Carlow
R747
N62
Freshford
Arklow
Suir
Barrow
Bagenalstown
N80
N11
Bunratty
N7
Thurles
N8
Kilkenny
Gorey
Limerick
Maddoxstown
Ferns
Adare
N24
N76
Borris
Enniscorthy
Ballingarry
Callan
N10
Thomastown
N30
Ballymurn
Tipperary
Cashel
New Ross
Ballsbridge
Cahir
Clonmel
N24
R733
Wexford
Kilmallock
Newcastle
Nire Valley
Campile
N25
Rosslare
N20
N8
R668
Ballymacarbry
Waterford
Arthurstown
Doneraile
Glencairn
Cappoquin
N25
Tagoat
Mallow
Blackwater
R675
Fermoy
N72
Mill Street
Dungarvan
N20
Castlelyons
Blarney
Youghal
Cork
Killeagh
Ardmore
Lee
Midleton
Farran
N27
Cobh
Shanagarry
N71
Kinsale
R600
Ballinspittle
Timoleage

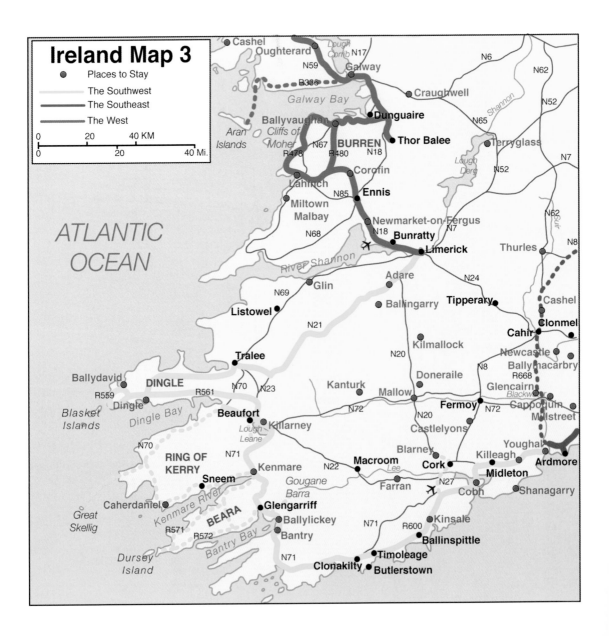

Ireland Map 3

- ● Places to Stay
- The Southwest
- The Southeast
- The West

0 — 20 — 40 KM
0 — 20 — 40 Mi.

ATLANTIC OCEAN

Cashel
Oughterard
Lough Corrib
N17
N59
Galway
N6
N62
Craughwell
R336
Galway Bay
Shannon
N52
Dunguaire
Aran Islands
Ballyvaughan
Cliffs of Moher
BURREN
N67
R478
R480
N18
Thor Balee
Terryglass
N65
Corofin
Lough Derg
N52
N7
Lahinch
N85
Ennis
Miltown Malbay
Newmarket-on-Fergus
N7
N62
N68
N18
Bunratty
River Shannon
Limerick
Thurles
N8
Suir
N69
Glin
Adare
N24
Tipperary
Cashel
Listowel
Ballingarry
Clonmel
N21
Cahir
Kilmallock
Newcastle
Ballymacarbry
N20
R668
Tralee
Kanturk
Mallow
Doneraile
Glencairn
Blackwater
N8
Ballydavid
DINGLE
R559
R561
N70
N23
N72
Fermoy
N72
Cappoquin
Dingle
Blasket Islands
Dingle Bay
Beaufort
Killarney
Castlelyons
N20
Millstreet
Lough Leane
Blarney
Youghal
N70
RING OF KERRY
N71
Kenmare
N22
Macroom
Lee
Cork
Killeagh
Ardmore
Sneem
Gougane Barra
Farran
Midleton
Shanagarry
Caherdaniel
Kenmare River
BEARA
Glengarriff
Cobh
Great Skellig
R571
R572
Ballylickey
Bantry
N71
Kinsale
R600
Ballinspittle
Dursey Island
Bantry Bay
N71
Timoleage
Clonakilty
Butlerstown

Ireland Map 4

● Places to Stay
— The Southwest
— The Southeast
▪▪▪ The North
— The West

0   20   40 KM
0   20   40 Mi.

ATLANTIC
OCEAN

Ballyshannon
N3
Lower
Lough
Erne
A32
Lisadell
N15
Drumcliff
A46
Enniskillen
A4
Ballycastle
Céide
Fields
R314
R315
N59
Sligo
N16
A4
A509
Upper
Lough
Erne
Clones
Crossmolina
N59
Riverstown
Ballymote
Lough
Allen
Kilmactranny
Cloverhill
N3
Achill
Island
R319
Rosturk
Lough
Conn
N26
N17
N4
Carrick on
Shannon
N3
N55
Castlebar
N5
N60
Castlerea
Longford
Lough
Sheelin
Clew
Bay
Westport
N60
N63
N55
Inny
N4
Croagh/
Patrick
Killary
Harbour
R335
N59
Lough
Mask
Lough
Ree
Mullingar
Inishbofin
Letterfrack
Leenane
N6
Clifden
CONNEMARA
Caherlistrane
N17
Lough
Corrib
N6
Ballynahinch
Cashel
Roundstone
R341
Oughterard
N59
N62
N52
N80
Galway
R336
Craughwell
Shannon
Aran
Islands
Galway Bay
Dunguaire
N65
Terryglass
Portlaoise
Ballyvaughan
Cliffs of
Moher
Thor Balee
N52
R478
N67
R480
BURREN
N18
Lough
Derg
N7
Corofin
Abbeyleix
Lahinch
N85
Ennis
Freshford
Miltown
Malbay
Newmarket-on-Fergus
N7
N62
N68
N18
Bunratty
Limerick
Thurles
N8
Kilkenny
River Shannon
Adare
N24
N76
Glin

IRELAND
2007

A farmhouse, Ring of Kerry

Contents

Beneta

you live on in the hearts of everyone

you touched and loved while you were here

Author: June Eveleigh Brown.

Editors: Anthony Brown, Clare Brown, Karen Brown, June Eveleigh Brown, Iris Sandilands, Debbie Tokumoto.

Illustrations: Barbara Maclurcan Tapp.

Cover painting: Jann Pollard.

Front photos: Connemara, Dublin doors, Back photo: Kinsale.

Maps: Michael Fiegel, Rachel Kircher-Randolph.

Technical support: Gary Meisner.

Copyright © 2007 by Karen Brown's Guides.

This book or parts thereof may not be reproduced in any form without obtaining written permission from the publisher: Karen Brown's Guides, P.O. Box 70, San Mateo, CA 94401, USA. Email: karen@karenbrown.com

Distributed by National Book Network, 15200 NBN Way, Blue Ridge Summit, PA 17214, USA. Tel: 717-794-3800 or 1-800-462-6420, Fax: 1-800-338-4500, Email: custserv@nbnbooks.com

A catalog record for this book is available from the British Library.

ISSN 1535-7341

Introduction

Writers wax lyrical about Ireland's spectacular scenery: ever-changing landscapes, splendid seascapes, purple moorlands, monastic ruins, enchanting lakes, towering fortresses, and vast, spreading patchworks of fields in every shade of green. Believe every word they say, but realize that it's the people with their open friendliness and warmth of welcome that make a visit to Ireland special. This guide is all about Irish hospitality and staying in places where you are a houseguest rather than a customer. Ireland is not conducive to rushing: the narrow country roads lend themselves to exploration at a leisurely pace where you return the smile and wave of greeting of those you pass. Take time to stop at a pub and be drawn into conversation, and when you get lost, ask directions and learn a bit of history or folklore as a bonus, along with the directions.

About This Guide

Ireland: Charming Inns & Itineraries is written specifically for independent travelers who want to experience a slice of Irish life staying as guests in country houses, farms, and family-run hotels. Our guide is not written for those who want the symmetry of worldwide, hotel chains with their identical bathrooms and mini-bars. The fondest memories of a visit to the Emerald Isle are those of its warm-hearted, friendly people, and there can be no better way to meet the Irish than to stay with them in their homes.

In the title, the term "inn" is generic for all types of lodgings ranging from a simple farmhouse bed & breakfast to a luxurious country estate, owned and run by a welcoming family. These are often the kinds of places where you are expected to carry your own bags. Service may not be the most efficient and occasionally the owners have their eccentricities, which all adds to the allure. There are enough recommendations in every price category to enable you to tailor your trip to your budget. We have recommended accommodation in the widest of price ranges, so please do not expect the same standard of luxury at, for example, Foxmount Farm, as The Park Hotel Kenmare—there is no comparison—yet each is outstanding in what it offers. Rates are quoted in euros in the Republic of Ireland and pounds sterling in Northern Ireland.

To keep you on the right track, we have formed itineraries linking the most interesting sightseeing, enabling you to spend from a few weeks to a month exploring this fascinating island. In addition, we have designed a walking tour of Dublin's fair city that blends culture, history, shopping, and Guinness.

Please supplement this book with the Karen Brown website (*www.karenbrown.com*). Our site contains not only a wealth of information for planning your vacation, but also post-press updates on our guides, and is a handy source for Michelin maps. A great many of the properties in this guide are featured there (their web addresses are on their description pages) with photos and direct links to their email and their own website.

About Ireland

The following pointers are given in alphabetical order, not in order of importance.

AIRFARE

Karen Brown's Guides have long recommended Auto Europe for their excellent car rental services. Their air travel division, Destination Europe, an airline broker working with major American and European carriers, offers deeply discounted coach- and business-class fares to over 200 European gateway cities. It also gives Karen Brown travelers an additional 5% discount off its already highly competitive prices (cannot be combined with any other offers or promotions). We recommend making reservations by phone at (800) 835-1555. When phoning, be sure to use the Karen Brown ID number 99006187 to secure your discount.

CLIMATE

It has been said that there is no such thing as climate in Ireland—only weather, and no such thing as bad weather—only the wrong clothes. This is because the changes in conditions from day to day, and even from hour to hour, seem greater than the changes from one season to the next. The Atlantic Ocean and the air masses moving east give Ireland very little seasonal variation in temperature, producing mild winters and cool summers. The ocean's influence is strongest near the coast, especially in winter when areas bordering the sea are milder than those inland. Coastal areas, particularly in the west, also have less variation in temperature between day and night. Even when it rains, and it does, it never pours—it's just soft Irish rain that keeps the isle emerald. The best thing is to be prepared for sun and sudden squalls at all times.

CLOTHING

Ireland is an easygoing place and casual clothes are acceptable everywhere, even at the fanciest restaurants. Because the weather is changeable, layers of sweaters and shirts that can be added to and removed are recommended. A lightweight, waterproof jacket with a hood is indispensable. Do not haul huge suitcases into bed & breakfasts; rather, we suggest that you have a small suitcase (the size that fits under your airline seat) that you take into the places you stay, leaving larger luggage in the car.

CURRENCY

The unit of currency in Northern Ireland is the pound sterling, while in the Republic of Ireland it is the euro. The two currencies do not have equal value. Visit our website (*www.karenbrown.com/news/currency.html*) for an online currency converter.

An increasingly popular and convenient way to obtain foreign currency is simply to use your bankcard at an ATM machine. You pay a fixed fee for this but, depending on the amount you withdraw, it is usually less than the percentage-based fee charged to exchange currency or travelers' checks. Be sure to check with your bank or credit card company about fees and necessary pin numbers prior to departure.

DRIVING

It is to the countryside that you must go, for to visit Ireland without driving through the country areas is to miss the best she has to offer. Driving is on the left-hand side of the road, which may take a little getting used to if you drive on the right at home, so avoid driving in cities until you feel comfortable with the system. If your arrival city is Dublin, do not pick your car up until you are ready to leave for the countryside. A valid driver's license from your home country is required. Your car will not be an automatic unless you specifically reserve one. Petrol (gasoline) is extremely expensive.

In the Republic, people usually do not use road numbers when giving directions: they refer to roads as where they might lead to (e.g., the Cork road). To add to the confusion, new road signs quote distances in kilometers, while old signs are in miles. The Irish seem to use neither, always quoting distances in the number of hours it takes them to drive.

The distances in Ireland are not great, but often the roads are not great either—though they are getting a lot better. Plan on being in a traffic jam every time a road goes through a town. Roads and motorways around Dublin are nearly always congested. Estimate your journey on the basis of an average of 30 miles (about 50 kilometers) per hour.

The types of roads found in Ireland are as follows:

MOTORWAYS: The letter "M" precedes these fast roads, which have two or three lanes of traffic either side of a central divider. Motorways are more prevalent in Northern Ireland though they are becoming more common between larger towns in the Republic.

NATIONAL ROADS: The letter "N" precedes the road number in the Republic, while in Northern Ireland, the road number is preceded by the letter "A." They are the straightest and most direct routes you can take when motorways are not available.

REGIONAL ROADS: The letter "R" precedes the road number on maps, but their numbers rarely, if ever, appear on signposts. They are usually wide enough for two cars or one tractor.

Off the major routes, road signs are not posted as often as you might wish, so when you drive it's best to plan some extra time for asking the way. Asking the way does have its advantages—you get to experience Irish directions from natives always ready to assure you that you cannot miss your destination—which gives you the opportunity of asking another friendly local the way when you do. One of the joys of meandering along less traveled country roads is rounding a bend to find that cows and sheep take precedence over cars as they saunter up the middle of the road.

DRIVING–CAR RENTAL

Readers frequently ask our advice on car rental companies. We always use Auto Europe—a car rental broker that works with the major car rental companies to find the lowest possible price. They also offer motor homes and chauffeur services. Auto Europe's toll-free phone service, from every European country, connects you to their U.S.-based, 24-hour reservation center (ask for the Europe Phone Numbers Card to be mailed to you). Auto Europe offers our readers a 5% discount (cannot be combined with any other offers or promotions) and, occasionally, free upgrades. Be sure to use the Karen Brown ID number 99006187 to receive your discount and any special offers. You can make your own reservations online via our website, *www.karenbrown.com* (select *Auto Europe* from the home page), or by phone (800-223-5555).

INFORMATION

The Irish Tourist Board (*bord failte*) and Northern Ireland Tourist Board are invaluable sources of information. Outside Ireland, they have combined their organizations under the auspices of "Tourism Ireland." They can supply you with details on all of Ireland and, on request, specific information on accommodation in homes, farmhouses, and manors; and information on festivals, fishing, and the like. The easiest way to contact them is via *www.tourismireland.com*. You can also reach them by phone as follows:

Australia: (0)2 9299 6177

Canada: (800) 223 6470

Great Britain: 0800 0397000

New Zealand: 0 9 977 2255

USA: (800) 669 9967

MAPS

Each of our driving itineraries is preceded by a map showing the route, and each hotel listing is referenced to a map at the front of the book. These are an artist's renderings and, although we have tried to include as much information as possible, you will need a more detailed map to plan your travels. Our preference is for the Michelin Map of Ireland, Map 712, where the scale is 1 centimeter to 4 kilometers (i.e. 1 inch to 6.3 miles), available in our website store at *www.karenbrown.com.*

PUBS

Ireland's pubs will not disappoint—if you do not expect sophisticated establishments. Most of the 12,000 pubs, where the Irish share ideas over frothing pints of ale and porter, have a contagious spirit and charm. Stop at a pub and you'll soon be drawn into conversation. At local pubs, musicians and dancers perform for their own enjoyment, their audience being those who stop by for a drink. If this kind of entertainment appeals to you, ask someone wherever you are staying to recommend a local pub that will have live music that night.

ROOTS

The Potato Famine of the 1840s cut population by a fourth. Through the lean decades that followed, the Irish left by the thousands to make new lives, primarily in the United States, Canada, Australia, and New Zealand. The first step in tracing your Irish roots is to collect together as much information on your Irish antecedent as possible, and to find out from relatives or documents (death or marriage certificates) just where he or she came from in Ireland. Armed with this information, your choices are several:

DO IT YOURSELF: If your ancestors hailed from Southern Ireland, visit the genealogical office on Kildare Street in Dublin. If your ancestors came from Northern Ireland, visit the Public Record Office of Northern Ireland, 66 Balmoral Avenue, Belfast BT9 6NY, which is open for visitors to do their own research.

HAVE SOMEONE DO IT FOR YOU: The Republic's genealogical office charges a small fee, but often has a backlog, so it takes time to do a general search. Write to Chief Herald, General Office of Ireland, 2 Kildare Street, Dublin 2, tel: (01) 603 0200, enclosing whatever information you have on your ancestors.

If your ancestors came from Northern Ireland, send information about them, along with a letter, to one of the following: General Register Office, Oxford House, 49 Chichester Street, Belfast BT1 4HL; Presbyterian Historical Society, Church House, Fisherwick Place, Belfast BT1 6DU.

The major tourist offices have brochures on tracing your ancestors that give more detailed information and provide information on publications that may be of interest to those of Irish descent.

SHOPPING

Prices of goods are fairly standard throughout Ireland, so make your purchases as you find items you like, since it is doubtful that you will find them again at a less expensive price. The most popular items to buy are hand-knitted sweaters, tweeds, crystal, china, and hand-embroidered linens.

Value Added Tax (VAT) is included in the price of your purchases. There is usually a minimum purchase requirement, but it is possible for visitors from non-EU countries to get a refund of the VAT on the goods they buy in one of two ways:

1. If the goods are shipped overseas direct from the point of purchase, the store can deduct the VAT at the time of sale.

2. Visitors taking the goods with them should ask the store to issue a VAT refund receipt. A passport is needed for identification. On departure, **before** you check in for your flight, go to the refund office at Shannon or Dublin airport. Your receipts will be stamped and they may ask to see your purchases. You will be given a cash refund in the currency of your choice.

About Itineraries

To keep you on the right track, we have created driving itineraries covering the most interesting sightseeing. If time allows, you can link the four itineraries together and travel all around Ireland. Each itinerary explores a region's scenic beauty, history, and culture, and avoids its large cities. Along the way, we suggest alternative routes and side trips (indicated in italics). At the beginning of each itinerary, we suggest our recommended pacing to help you decide the amount of time to allocate to each region. Do not try to see all of Ireland in a week—this is frankly impossible. You will enjoy yourself much more if you concentrate on a smaller number of destinations and stay for at least a couple of nights in each, rather than spending most of your precious vacation rushing from place to place. The capricious changes in the weather mean that often what appears sparkling and romantic in sunshine, appears dull and depressing under gathering storm clouds. If the weather is stormy, find a nice place to stay with good company. Once the rain clears, there is much to see. Each itinerary is preceded by an artist's rendering of the proposed route, and outlined on the color maps at the front of the book. We suggest that you outline this on a commercial map: our preference is the Michelin Map of Ireland where the scale is 1 centimeter to 4 kilometers (1/400,000).

Overview Map: Driving Itineraries

The North

Rosgull Peninsula

Tory Island

Giant's Causeway

Glencolumbkille

Donegal

Belfast

The West

Céide Fields

Sligo

Lough Gill

Achill
Island

Crossmolina

Inishbofin
Island

Connemara

Clifden

Galway

Dublin

Dublin
Walking
Tour

Burren

Aran
Islands

Kilkenny

Limerick

Dingle Peninsula

Cashel

Waterford

The Southeast

Killarney

Blarney

Ring
of Kerry

Kenmare

Skellig Michael

Cork

Youghal

Itinerary Route

Alternative Routes
& Sidetrips

Kinsale

Beara Peninsula

The Southwest

About Places to Stay

This book does not cover the many, modern hotels in Ireland with their look-alike bedrooms, televisions, and direct-dial phones. Rather, it offers a selection of personally recommended lodgings that cover the widest range, from a very basic, clean room in a simple farmhouse to a sumptuous suite in an elegant, castle hotel. In some, the decor is less than perfect, but the one thing they all have in common is that their owners offer wholehearted hospitality. We have inspected each and every one, and have stayed in a great many. The accommodations selected are the kind of places that we enjoy. We have tried to be candid and honest in our appraisals and to convey each listing's special flavor so that you know what to expect and will not be disappointed. To help you appreciate and understand what to expect when staying at listings in this guide, the following pointers are given in alphabetical order, not in order of importance.

CHILDREN

The majority of listings in this guide welcome children. A great many places offer family rooms with a double and one or two single beds in a room. If you want to tuck your children up in bed and enjoy a leisurely dinner, many of the listings will—with advance notice—provide an early supper for children.

CHRISTMAS

If the information section indicates that the listing is open during the Christmas holiday season, there is a very good chance that it offers a festive Christmas package.

Introduction: About Places to Stay

CREDIT CARDS

Whether or not an establishment accepts credit cards is indicated in the list of icons at the bottom of each description by the symbol ▨. We have also specified in the accommodation description which cards are accepted as follows: none, AX–American Express, MC–MasterCard, VS–Visa, or simply, all major.

DIRECTIONS

We give concise driving directions to guide you to the listing, which is often in a more out-of-the-way place than the town or village in the address. We would be very grateful if you would let us know of cases where our directions have proven inadequate.

ELECTRICITY

The voltage is 240. Most hotels, guesthouses, and farmhouses have American-style razor points for 110 volts. If you are coming from overseas, it is recommended that you take only dual-voltage appliances and a kit of electrical plugs. Your host can usually loan you a hairdryer or an iron.

HANDICAP FACILITIES

If there is *at least* one guestroom that is accessible by wheelchair, it is noted with the symbol ♿. This is not the same as saying it meets full disability standards. In reality, it can be anything from a basic ground-floor room to a fully equipped facility. Please discuss your requirements when you call your chosen place to stay to see if they have accommodation that is suitable for you.

HIDDEN IRELAND

Several of the listings are members of Hidden Ireland, a consortium of private houses that open their doors to a handful of guests at a time. All houses are of architectural merit and character with owners to match. These are the kinds of houses where you can indulge yourself by staying with people who have mile-long driveways, grand dining rooms watched over by redoubtable ancestors, four-poster beds that you have to climb into, and vast billiard rooms. The kinds of places most of us can only dream of living in, but where you are very welcome as guests because you are the ones who help the owners pay their central heating bills, school fees, and gardeners. Guests become a part of the household and family life carries on around you—you are not expected to scuttle up to your room. Everyone usually dines together round a polished table and, unless you make special requests, you eat what is served to you. The conversation flows and you meet people you might never have met elsewhere. Early or late in the season, you may find that you are the only guests and you can enjoy a romantic, candlelit dinner in a house full of character and charm. There are lakes full of salmon and stylish modern bedrooms at Delphi, gigantic old-fashioned bedrooms at Temple House, homey friendliness at Lorum Old Rectory, and delightful thematically decorated bedrooms at Quay House. When a property is a member of this group, we note it at the bottom of the description.

ICONS

We use these icons in the guidebooks and more on our website, *www.karenbrown.com.*
❄ Air conditioning in rooms, ☕ Breakfast included in room rate, ☃ Children welcome
(age given on website), ⚗ Cooking classes offered, [CREDIT] Credit cards accepted, ☎
Direct-dial telephone in room, ⛰ Dinner served upon request, ☖ Dogs by special
request, ⛩ Elevator, ☗ Exercise room, ☡ Mini-refrigerator in room, ⊘ Non-smoking
rooms, **P** Parking available, ⑂ Restaurant, ☗ Room service, ☘ Spa, ⚑ Swimming
pool, ⚼ Tennis, ▣ TV in bedrooms, ☙ Wedding facilities, ♿ Wheelchair accessible,
♈ Beach nearby, ⚐ Golf course nearby, ☖ Hiking trails nearby, ☗ Horseback riding
nearby, ⚐ Skiing nearby, ☗ Water sports nearby. Icons allow us to provide additional
information about our recommended properties. When using our website to supplement
the guides, positioning the cursor over an icon will, in many cases, give you further
details.

IRELAND'S BLUE BOOK

Several of our listings are members of the Irish Country Houses Association, usually
referred to as The Blue Book because of the distinctive blue color of its brochure. This is
an association of owner-managed country houses, hotels, and restaurants. The majority
are country house hotels offering accommodation in charming surroundings with
restaurants, bars, and room service. However, there are several members who welcome
guests to their ancestral homes on house-party lines (much as members of Hidden
Ireland) with no bar and a set dinner menu. When a property is a member of this group,
we note it at the bottom of the description.

MAPS

At the front of the book are four regional maps showing each recommended place to stay's location. The pertinent regional map number is given at the right on the top line of each accommodation's description.

MEALS

Owners of guesthouses, farmhouses, and bed & breakfasts are often happy to serve an evening meal, if you make arrangements 24 hours in advance. Country houses offer a set menu of more elaborate fare and most offer interesting wines—again, arrangements to dine must be made 24 hours in advance. Whether or not an establishment offers dinner is indicated in the list of icons at the bottom of each description by the symbol 🔔. **You cannot just arrive and expect dinner.** Hotels and restaurants offer menus and wine lists, giving you more dining choices. If an establishment has a restaurant we indicate it with a 🍴. Our suggestion is that you make arrangements for dinner on the night of your arrival at the same time as you make reservations for accommodation.

RATES

Rates are those quoted to us, either verbally or by correspondence, for the 2007 high season (June, July, and August). The rates given generally cover the least expensive to the most expensive double room (two people sharing a room) inclusive of taxes and, in most cases, breakfast. We do not quote rates for a single person occupying a room. When a listing does not include breakfast in its rates, we mention this in the description. We feel a great deal of resentment when an obligatory service charge of 10–15% is added to the bill, and feel that establishments often use this as a way of padding their rates. Forewarned is forearmed, so we have indicated if an establishment adds a service charge. Please **always check** prices and terms when making a reservation. Rates are quoted in euros in the Republic of Ireland and pounds sterling in Northern Ireland. Prices vary considerably and, on the whole, reflect the type of house in which you will be staying.

From the charm of a simple farmhouse to the special ambiance of a vast sporting estate, each listing reflects the Irish way of life.

RESERVATIONS

When making your reservations, be sure to identify yourself as a "Karen Brown Traveler." The hotels appreciate your visit, value their inclusion in our guide, frequently tell us they take special care of our readers, and many offer special rates to Karen Brown members (visit our website at *www.karenbrown.com*). We hear over and over again that the people who use our guides are such wonderful guests!

It is important to understand that once reservations for accommodation are confirmed, whether verbally by phone or in writing, you are under contract. This means that the proprietor is obligated to provide the accommodation that was promised, and that you are obligated to pay for it. If you cannot, you are liable for a portion of the accommodation charges plus your deposit. Although some proprietors do not strictly enforce a cancellation policy many, particularly the smaller properties in our book, simply cannot afford not to do so. Similarly, many airline tickets cannot be changed or refunded without penalty. We recommend insurance to cover these types of additional expenses arising from cancellation due to unforeseen circumstances. A link on our website (*www.karenbrown.com*) will connect you to a variety of insurance policies that can be purchased online.

Reservations should always be made in advance for Dublin accommodation. In the countryside, space is not so tight and a room can often be had simply by calling in the morning. July and August are the busiest times and if you are traveling to a popular spot, you should make advance reservations. Be specific as to what your needs are, such as a ground-floor room, en suite shower, twin beds, family room. Check the prices, which may well have changed from those given in the book (summer 2007). Ask what deposit to send or give your credit card number. Tell them about what time you intend to arrive and request dinner if you want it. There are several options for making reservations.

Introduction: About Places to Stay

EMAIL: This is our preferred way of making a reservation. If the hotel/bed & breakfast is on our website and has email, its web page contains a link to its email. (Always spell out the month as the Irish reverse the American month/day numbering system.)

FAX: If you have access to a fax machine, this is a very quick way to reach a hotel/bed & breakfast. If the place to stay has a fax, we have included the number in the listing. (See EMAIL above about spelling out the month.)

LETTER: If you write for reservations, you will usually receive your confirmation and a map. You should then send your deposit. (See comment on EMAIL about spelling out month.)

TELEPHONE: By telephoning you have your answer immediately, so if space is not available, you can then decide on an alternative. If calling from the United States, allow for the time difference (Ireland is five hours ahead of New York) so that you can call during their business day. Dial 011 (the international code), 353 (Republic of Ireland's code) **or** 44 (Northern Ireland's code), then the city code (dropping the 0), and the telephone number.

SELF-CATERING ACCOMMODATION

An excellent way to explore an area is to rent self-catering accommodation on a weekly basis. You can unpack your bags, put your feet up and make yourself at home, come and go as you please, and eat what you like when you like. Tir Na Fiúise in Terryglass is our only exclusively self-catering properties. Several of the country houses that operate as bed & breakfasts can be rented in their entirety as luxurious homes. A great many listings have additional houses, cottages, and converted outbuildings that range from former coach houses to a one-time hen house. Because our primary focus is on beds, breakfasts, and evening meals, we often do not have space to discuss self-catering accommodation at length. We quote a range of rates: from the smallest unit in the low season to the largest unit in the high season, on a weekly or daily basis. Please discuss your requirements when contacting owners to see if they have accommodation that is suitable for you.

SIGHTSEEING

We have tried to mention sightseeing attractions near each lodging to encourage you to spend several nights in each location.

WEBSITE

Please visit the Karen Brown website (*www.karenbrown.com*) in conjunction with this book. It provides comments and discoveries from you, our readers, information on our latest finds, post-press updates, the opportunity to purchase goods and services that we recommend (airline tickets, rail tickets, car rental, travel insurance), and one-stop shopping for our guides and associated maps. Most of our favorite places to stay participate in our website, where you can find color photos and direct links to their own websites and email.

Dublin Walking Tour·

Dublin Writers Museum

To Balgriffin

Parnell Square

Gate Theatre

Dublin Tourism Office

Connoly Station

GPO

Customs House

To Bullock Harbour →

O'Connell Bridge

River Liffey

Four Courts

Dublina

Christ Church

Bank of Ireland

Trinity College

Dublin Castle

Powerscourt Townhouse

← To Guinness Brewery

National Gallery

St Patrick's Cathedral

Merrion Square

St. Stephen's Green

Number 29

Newman House

To Bray and Wicklow

To Ballsbridge

KEY

1. Belcamp Hutchinson
2. The Clarence
3. The Merrion
4. Harrington Hall
5. Kilronan House
6. Number 31
7. Mespil Hotel
8. Waterloo House
▪▪▪▪ Walking Tour

19

Dublin Walking Tour

"In Dublin's fair city, where the girls are so pretty . . ." goes the popular old ballad. The girls are certainly pretty and the city fair, if you can overlook the rash of modern office developments begun in the 1960s and the areas that have been razed and seemingly abandoned. Dublin now appears to have seen the error of its ways and efforts are being made to restore what the bulldozers have spared. A car is more trouble than it is worth in Dublin. If your visit here is at the outset of your trip, we suggest that you not get your car until you are ready to leave or—if Dublin is a stop on your trip—park it for the duration of your stay. Dublin is a walking town, so don comfortable shoes and set out to explore the buildings, streets, and shops of this bustling, friendly city. If you feel weary along the way, there is no shortage of pubs where you can revive yourself with a refreshing drink.

Recommended Pacing: If you select a few museums that appeal to you and simply skirt the exterior of the others, this walking tour can be accomplished in a day, which means that you will need two nights' accommodation in Dublin.

Make your first stop the **Dublin Tourism Centre**, in a sturdy, granite church on Suffolk Street. Here you can book sightseeing tours; purchase ferry, train, and bus tickets; arrange lodgings; find out what is in Dublin—and enjoy a cup of coffee. (*Tel: 01 605 7720, www.visitdublin.com.*) Dublin is easily explored on foot, but as an introduction take one of the double-decker sightseeing buses. The tours run every ten minutes and wind a circular route through the city with a commentary on the significance of the buildings along the route. Your ticket is valid for twenty-four hours. The bus makes frequent stops so you can take the entire tour for an overview of what there is to see and then later use it as transportation between the sights, hopping on and off to visit the places that interest you.

Our walking tour begins at the southern end of O'Connell Street where **O'Connell Bridge** spans the River Liffey dividing the north from the south of Dublin. (It is also just by the city center terminus for buses: those displaying "*An Lar,*" meaning city center, usually end up here.) Turn south into **Westmoreland Street** past the somber, windowless **Bank of Ireland**, which began life in 1729 as the seat of the Irish parliament. Cross the street and enter through the front arch of **Trinity College** into the cobbled square. Founded in 1591 by Elizabeth I, it contains a fine collection of buildings from the 18th to the 20th centuries. Cross the square to the library, where a display center houses the jewel of Trinity College, the ***Book of Kells,*** a Latin text of the Four Gospels. A page of this magnificent, illuminated manuscript is turned every month and if you are not overly impressed by the page on display, return to the library bookshop and browse through a reproduction. (*Open daily.*) While at the college visit **The Dublin Experience**, a sophisticated audio-visual presentation that orients you to the main events of Irish history. (*Open end of May–Sep.*)

Retrace your steps to the front gate and turn south into pedestrians-only **Grafton Street**, teeming with people and enlivened by street musicians. Its large, department store, **Brown Thomas**, is popular with visitors.

At the end of Grafton Street, dodge the hurrying buses and cross into the peaceful tranquility of **St. Stephen's Green**, an island of flowers, trees, and grass surrounding small lakes dotted with ducks. On the far side of the square, at 85 and 86 St. Stephen's Green, is **Newman House**, once the home of the old Catholic University (later University College Dublin), which boasted James Joyce amongst its distinguished graduates. Number 85 is restored to its pristine, aristocratic years of the 1740s. On the ground floor are wall reliefs of the god Apollo and his nine muses, done elaborately in stucco. A staircase of Cuban mahogany leads to a reception room with more riotous plasterwork figures on the ceiling. Number 86 has some rooms with interesting associations with the Whaley family and Gerard Manley Hopkins, and the Bishop's Room has been restored to its Victorian splendor. (*Open Jun, Jul, Aug, tours on the hour from noon, tel: 01 706 7422.*)

Return to the north side of the square to the landmark **Shelbourne Hotel**, long recommended as the perfect place to enjoy afternoon tea. Follow **Merrion Row** and turn left into **Merrion Street** passing the back of **Leinster House**, the Irish Parliament. It consists of two chambers—the *Dáil*, the lower house, and the *Seanad*, the upper house or senate. You can tour the building when parliament is not in session. Adjacent to the parliament building is the **National Gallery of Ireland**, which is a Victorian building with about 3,000 works of art. There's a major collection of Ireland's greatest painter, Jack Yeats, and works by Canaletto, Goya, Titian, El Greco, Poussin, Manet, Picasso, and many others. (*Open daily, tel: 01 661 5133, website: www.nationalgallery.ie.*)

Merrion Square is one of Dublin's finest remaining Georgian squares and the onetime home of several famous personages—William Butler Yeats lived at 82 and earlier at 52, Daniel O'Connell at 51, and Oscar Wilde's parents occupied number 1. The jewel of Merrion Square is **Number 29** Lower Fitzwilliam Street (corner of Lower Fitzwilliam

Street and Upper Mount Street), a magnificently restored, late 18th-century townhouse. From the basement through living rooms to the nursery and playroom, the house is meticulously furnished in the style of the period 1790–1820. (*Closed Mon, tel: 01 702 6165.*)

Stroll into **Clare Street**, stopping to browse in **Greene's Bookstore** with its lovely, old façade and tables of books outside.

Detour into **Kildare Street**, where you find the **National Museum** displaying all the finest treasures of the country. There are marvelous examples of gold, bronze, and other ornaments, as well as relics of the Viking occupation of Dublin—the 8th-century Tara Brooch is perhaps the best-known item here.

Merrion Square

Follow the railings of Trinity College to the **Kilkenny Design Centre** and **Blarney Woolen Mills**, fine places to shop for Irish crafts and clothing.

With your back to the front gate of Trinity College, cross into **Dame Street**, where the statue of Henry Grattan, a famous orator, stands with arms outstretched outside the parliament building. Walk along Dame Street past Dublin's most famous 1960s "modern" building, the **Central Bank**, which looks like egg boxes on stilts. Go under the bank and you are in **Temple Bar**, with its narrow cobbled streets and little old buildings. In the daytime it's a place of coffee houses and little shops. At night its narrow streets become very vibrant as the clubs open with many good pubs and lots of restaurants—a favorite place for young people. Returning to Dame Street and a more sedate side of Dublin, you come to **Dublin Castle**, built in the early 13th century on the site of an earlier Danish fortification. The adjoining 18th-century **State Apartments** with their ornate furnishings are more impressive inside than out. (*Open daily, tel: 01 677 7129.*)

Returning to Dame Street, you pass **City Hall** and, on your right, the impressive **Christ Church Cathedral** comes into view. Dedicated in 1192, it has been rebuilt and restored many times. After the Reformation when the Protestant religion was imposed on the Irish people, it became a Protestant cathedral (Church of Ireland). The large crypt remained as a gathering spot and marketplace for the locals (Catholics) who used it for many years, until a rector expelled them because their rowdiness was interrupting church services. Another point of interest is **Strongbow's Tomb**: he was one of the most famous Norman lords of Ireland and, by tradition, debts were paid across his tomb. When a wall collapsed and crushed it, a replacement—an unknown crusader's tomb—was conscripted and named Strongbow's Tomb. (*Open daily, tel: 01 677 8099.*)

Joined to the cathedral by a covered bridge arching across the street is **Dublina**, where you learn the history of Dublin through an audio-visual display. You conclude your tour at the large-scale model of the city and the gift shop. (*Open daily, tel: 01 679 4611.*)

At the junction of High Street and Bridge Street, pause to climb the restored remains of a portion of **Dublin's Walls**. When they were built in 1240, the walls fronted onto the River Liffey.

Just down **Thomas Street** is that thriving Dublin institution, the **Guinness Brewery**, whence flows the national drink. As you near your goal, the smell of roasting grains permeates the air. The Guinness Storehouse, a 7-story glass atrium, is built on the site where Arthur Guinness first signed his 9000-year brewery lease in 1759. Journey through the history of the brewing process, learn the story of the Guinness family, and end your tour with a pint of the black stuff in the Gravity bar with its panoramic views of the city. Of course there are lots of opportunities to purchase souvenirs of all-things Guinness. (*Open daily, tel: 01 408 4800.*)

If you decide not to visit the Guinness Brewery, cross diagonally from the walls to the **Brazen Head** in **Bridge Street**, where you can enjoy that same brew in Dublin's oldest pub. There has been a tavern on this site since Viking times, though the present, rather dilapidated, premises date from 1688. It's always a crowded spot that comes alive late in the evening, when musicians gather for impromptu sessions of traditional music.

Cross the River Liffey and, strolling along the **Inns Quay**, you come to the **Four Courts**, the supreme and high courts of Ireland. You can look inside the fine, circular waiting hall under the beautiful green dome, which allows light through its apex.

Turn left up **Capel Street** and make the third right into **Mary Street** which leads to the busiest pedestrian shopping street in Dublin, **Henry Street**. A short detour down **Moore Street** takes you through Dublin's colorful open-air fruit, vegetable, and flower market.

On reaching **O'Connell Street**, turn left. O'Connell Street has its share of tourist traps and hamburger stores, but it's a lively bunch of Dubliners who walk its promenades—placard-carrying nuns, nurses collecting for charity, hawkers of fruit, flowers, and plastic trinkets—all are there for you to see as you stroll along this wide boulevard and continue past the **Gate Theatre** into **Parnell Square**. At the north end of the square in a restored

18th-century mansion, you find the **Dublin Writers Museum**, where you can view the paintings and memorabilia with an audio tape telling you all about them. Among those featured are George Bernard Shaw, William Butler Yeats, Oscar Wilde, James Joyce, and Samuel Beckett. (*Open daily, tel: 01 872 2077.*)

Retrace your steps down O'Connell Street to the **General Post Office**. The GPO, as it is affectionately known, is a national shrine known as the headquarters of the 1916 revolution. Pass the statue of Daniel O'Connell and the millennium "spike" and you are back at your starting point, O'Connell Bridge.

Four Courts

Dublin Walking Tour

The Southeast

- ● Orientation/Sightseeing
- -- Itinerary Route
- — Roads
- ··· Alternative Route & Sidetrips
- ✈ Airport

Dublin
Howth
Powerscourt Gardens & Waterfall
Sally Gap
Rathnew
Glendalough
Annamoe
Wicklow
Vale of Avoca
Avoca
Arklow
Gorey
Kilkenny
R693
Freshford
Ferns
Enniscorthy
Cashel
New Ross
Cahir
N24
Wexford
Waterford
John F. Kennedy Park
Arthurstown
The Vee
Passage East
Lismore
N25
Tramore
N72
Dungarven
N25
Youghal
Cork
N25
N8
N9
N11

Belfast
Dublin

The Southeast

All too often visitors rush from Dublin through Waterford and on to western Ireland, never realizing that they are missing some of the most ancient antiquities and lovely scenery along the seductive little byways that traverse the moorlands and wind through wooded glens. This itinerary travels from Dublin into the Wicklow Mountains, pausing to admire the lovely Powerscourt Gardens, lingering amongst the ancient monastic ruins of Glendalough, visiting the Avoca handweavers who capture the subtle hues of heather and field in their fabric, and admiring the skill of the Waterford crystal cutters.

Glendalough

The Southeast

Recommended Pacing: If you are not a leisurely sightseer, and leave Dublin early, you can follow this itinerary and be in Youghal by nightfall. But resist the temptation—select a base for two nights in two places and explore at leisure. If you are not continuing westward and returning to Dublin via The Vee, Cashel, and Kilkenny, select a place to stay near Cashel or Kilkenny.

Leave Dublin following the N11 in the direction of Wexford. (If you have difficulty finding the correct road, follow signs for the ferry at Dun Laoghaire and, from there, pick up signs for Wexford.) As soon as the city suburbs are behind you, the road becomes a dual carriageway. Watch for signs indicating an exit signposted **Enniskerry** and **Powerscourt Gardens**. Follow the winding, wooded lane to Enniskerry and bear left in the center of the village. This brings you to the main gates of Powerscourt Gardens. As you drive through the vast, parklike grounds, the mountains of Wicklow appear before you, decked in every shade of green. Powerscourt House was burnt to a ruin in 1974: a rook's nest blocked one of the chimneys, and when a fire was lit in the fireplace, the resultant blaze quickly engulfed this grand home. Restoration is under way and, while there are no grand rooms to visit, you can enjoy refreshments at the restaurant and shopping at the Avoca knitwear store. The gardens descend in grand tiers from the ruined house, as if descending into a bowl—a mirror-like lake sits at the bottom. Masses of roses adorn the walled garden and velvet, green, grassy walks lead through the woodlands. Many visitors are intrigued by the animal cemetery with its little headstones and inscriptions—not an uncommon sight in Irish stately homes. (*Open mid-Mar–Oct, tel: 01 204 6000, email: gardens@powerscourt.ie, website: www.powerscourt.ies.*) Leaving the car park, turn left for the 6-kilometer drive to the foot of **Powerscourt Waterfall**, the highest waterfall in Ireland and a favorite summer picnic place for many Dubliners.

Turn to the left as you leave the waterfall grounds to meander along narrow country lanes towards **Glencree**. As you come upon open moorland, take the first turn left for the 8-kilometer uphill drive to the summit of **Sally Gap**. This road is known as the "old military road" because it follows the path that the British built across these wild mountains to aid them in their attempts to suppress the feisty men of County Wicklow.

Powerscourt Gardens

Neat stacks of turf are piled to dry in the sun. Grazing sheep seem to be the only occupants of this vast, rolling moorland. Below **Glenmacnass Waterfall**, the valley opens up to a patchwork of fields beckoning you to **Laragh** and Glendalough.

Glendalough, a monastic settlement of seven churches, was founded by St. Kevin in the 6th century. After St. Patrick, St. Kevin is Ireland's most popular saint. He certainly picked a stunning site in this wooded valley between two lakes to found his monastic order. Amidst the tilting stones of the graveyard, the round tower—still perfect after more than a thousand years—punctuates the skyline. The Interpretive Centre presents a 15-minute movie and display on the history of the area. (*Open all year, tel: 0404 45325.*) Take time to follow the track beyond Glendalough to the Upper Lake (you can also drive there). Tradition has it that St. Kevin lived a solitary life in a hut near here. Farther up on a cliff face is a cave known as St. Kevin's Bed. Here, so the story goes, Kathleen—a

The Southeast

beautiful temptress—tried to seduce the saint who, to cool her advances, threw her into the lake.

Retrace the road to Laragh, turn right, and travel south through the village of Rathdrum where sturdy stone cottages line the street, and continue through the crossroad following signposts for **Avondale House**, the home of Charles Stewart Parnell. Parnell was born into the ruling Anglo-Irish gentry; but, due in part to the influence of his more open-minded mother, an American, he became the leading light in Ireland's political fight for independence. His downfall was his long-term affair with a married English lady. The house is sparsely furnished and takes just a few minutes to tour. You can also wander around the estate with its wonderful trees. (*Open mid-Mar–Oct, tel: 0404 46111.*)

Leave Avondale to the left and you soon join the main road that takes you through the **Vale of Avoca** to the "Meeting of the Waters" at the confluence of the rivers Avonmore and Avonbeg. Detour into **Avoca** to visit the **Avoca Handweavers**. You are welcome to wander amongst the skeins and bobbins of brightly hued wool to see the weavers at work and talk to them above the noise of the looms. An adjacent shop sells tweeds and woolens. (*Open daily all year, tel: 01 286 7466.*)

At **Arklow** join the N11, a broad, fast road taking you south through Gorey and Ferns to **Enniscorthy**. Amidst the gray stone houses, built on steeply sloping ground by the River Slaney, lies a Norman castle. Rebuilt in 1586, the castle houses a folk museum that includes exhibits from the Stone Age to the present day, with emphasis on the part played by local people in the 1798 rebellion against English rule. (*Open all year, tel: 054 35926.*)

Take the N30 towards Waterford and just before **New Ross**, turn left towards Arthurstown. After about 1 kilometer, turn right for the **Kennedy Homestead** in **Dunganstown**, where the great-grandfather of American President John F. Kennedy lived before being driven from Ireland by the terrible potato famine of the 1840s. His simple, family cottage has been rather overly restored, but the rural location has changed little since the American branch of the family left Ireland. Interestingly, the farm is still owned by a Kennedy. (*Tel: 051 388264, email info@kennedyhomestead.com.*) Leaving the homestead, continue along the country lane to the main road and the **John F. Kennedy Arboretum**, a memorial to the slain president of row upon row of trees. (*Open all year, tel: 051 388171.*)

Leave the arboretum towards Arthurstown and, at the first Y in the road, take the right-hand fork for the short drive to Great Island and **Kilmokea** at **Campile** with its 7 acres of lovely gardens. Around the house are the formal, walled gardens and a heavy, wooden door set into the stone wall leading you to the winding paths of the woodland garden. Enjoy an excellent lunch or afternoon tea in the conservatory tearoom, and ask for directions for the short cut down narrow lanes to **Arthurstown**, where the **Passage East ferry** takes you across the estuary to **Passage East**, the tiny village on the western shores of Waterford harbor. Arriving at the N25, you turn right to visit the town of **Waterford** fronting the River Suir, and left to arrive at the **Waterford Crystal Factory**. This is a very worthwhile excursion, as the tours give you an appreciation for why these hand-blown, hand-cut items are so expensive. It takes many years to become a master craftsman, and one little mistake in the intricate cutting means painstaking hours of work are wasted and the defective item is simply smashed and recycled—there are no seconds. (Waterford crystal items are uniformly priced throughout the country.) It is a very popular venue, the stopping place for seemingly every coach tour. Fortunately, separate transportation is provided to shuttle individual tourists to and from the factory. I thoroughly enjoyed touring with a guide who allowed plenty of time to watch the skilled workmen. The showroom displays the full line of Waterford's production, from shimmering chandeliers to sparkling stemware. The visitors' center also has a gift shop, tourist information center, and café. (*Open daily, tel: 051 332500, fax: 051 332716, www.waterfordvisitorscentre.com.*)

If the weather is inclement, stay on the N25 in the direction of Cork, but otherwise meander along the coast road by doubling back in the direction of Waterford for a **very short** distance, turning to the right to **Tramore**, a family holiday town, long a favorite of the "ice-cream-and-bucket-and-spade" brigade. Skirting the town, follow the beautiful coastal road through **Annestown** to **Dungarvan**.

Where the coastal road meets the N25, detour from your route, turning sharp left to **Shell House**. Like it or hate it, there is nothing quite like it on any suburban street in the world—a cottage where all available wall surfaces are decorated with colored shells in various patterns.

Returning to the main road after crossing Dungarvan harbor, the N25 winds up and away from the coast, presenting lovely views of the town and the coast. If you haven't eaten, try **Seanachie** (a restored, thatched farmhouse, now a traditional restaurant and bar), which sits atop the hill and serves good Irish and Continental food. After passing through several kilometers of forests, turn left on the R673 to **Ardmore**, following the coastline to the village. Beyond the neatly painted houses clustered together lies the **Ardmore Monastic Site**. The well-preserved round tower used to have six internal timber landings joined by ladders, and at the top was a bell to call the monks to prayer or warn of a hostile raid. The round tower is unique to Ireland, its entrance door placed well above the ground: entry was gained by means of a ladder, which could be drawn up whenever necessary. Early Christian monks built round towers as protection against Vikings and other raiders. Leaving the ruins, turn left in the village for **Youghal** where this itinerary ends. Sightseeing in Youghal is outlined in the following itinerary. From Youghal you can continue west to follow *The Southwest* itinerary, or take the following alternative route back to Dublin via The Vee, Cashel, and Kilkenny.

Youghal

The Southeast

ROUTE FROM YOUGHAL TO DUBLIN VIA THE VEE, CASHEL, AND KILKENNY

From Youghal, retrace your steps towards Waterford to the bridge that crosses the River Blackwater, and turn sharp left (before you cross the river) on **Blackwater Valley Drive**, a narrow road which follows the broad, muddy waters of the Blackwater through scenic wooded countryside. The "drive" is well-signposted as "Scenic Route." Quiet country roads bring you into **Lismore**. Turn left into town and right at the town square. Cross the river and take the second road to the left, following signs for **Clogheen** and **The Vee**. As the road climbs, woods give way to heathery moorlands climbing to the summit where the valley opens before you—a broad "V" shape framing an endless patchwork of fields in every shade of green.

Continue on to **Cahir Castle**, which has stood on guard to defend the surrounding town of **Cahir** since 1375. A guided tour explains the elaborate defensive system, making a visit here both interesting and informative. A separate audio-visual presentation provides information about the castle and other monuments in the area. (*Open Oct–May, closed Mon, tel: 052 41011.*)

Leaving the castle, continue through the town square for the 16-kilometer drive to **Cashel**. The **Rock of Cashel** seems to grow out of the landscape as you near the town and you can see why this easily defensible site was the capital for the kings of Munster as long ago as 370 A.D. In the course of converting Ireland to Christianity, St. Patrick reached the castle and, according to legend, jabbed his staff into the king's foot during the conversion ceremony. The king apparently took it all very stoically, thinking it was part of the ritual. Upon reaching the summit of the rock, you find a 10th-century round tower, a 13th-century cathedral, and a 15th-century entrance building or Hall of Vicars Choral—a building which was sensitively restored in the 1970s and now houses some exhibits including St. Patrick's Cross, an ancient Irish high cross of unusual design. (*Open all year, tel: 062 61437.*) If you overnight in or near Cashel, be sure to enjoy **BrúBorú**, a foot-tapping evening of traditional Irish entertainment in the theater below the Rock. (*Jun–Sep, Tue–Sat, 9 pm, tel: 062 61122, fax: 062 62700.*)

Rock of Cashel

Leave Cashel on the N8 for the 40-kilometer drive northeast to **Urlingford**, where you bear right through **Freshford** for the 27-kilometer drive to **Kilkenny** (see listings). Kilkenny is quite the loveliest of Irish towns and it is easy to spend a day here sightseeing and shopping. Entering the town, turn left at the first traffic lights along the main street and park your car outside the castle.

Kilkenny Castle was originally built between 1195 and 1207. The imposing building, as it now stands, is a mixture of Tudor and Gothic design and is definitely worth a visit. The east wing picture gallery is flooded by natural light from the skylights in the roof and displays a collection of portraits of the Ormonde family, the owners of Kilkenny Castle from 1391 until 1967. (*Open all year, tel: 056 21450.*)

Opposite the castle entrance, the stables now house the **Kilkenny Design Centre**, a retail outlet for goods of Irish design and production: silver jewelry, knits, textiles, furniture, and crafts.

Undoubtedly, the best way to see the medieval buildings of Kilkenny is on foot. A walking tour starts from the tourist office in the **Shee Alms House**, just a short distance from the castle. Stroll up High Street into Parliament Street to **Rothe House**. The house, built in 1594 as the home of Elizabethan merchant John Rothe, is now a museum depicting how such a merchant lived. You should also see **St. Canice's Cathedral** at the top of Parliament Street. The round tower dates from the 6th century, when St. Canice founded a monastic order here. Building began on the cathedral in 1251, though most of the lovely church you see today is an 1864 restoration.

Alleyways, with fanciful names such as The Butter Slip, lead you from the High Street to St. Kieran Street where you find **Kylters Inn**, the oldest building in town. This historic inn has a lurid history—supposedly a hostess of many centuries ago murdered four successive husbands, was then accused of witchcraft, and narrowly escaped being burnt at the stake by fleeing to the Continent.

This is an area noted for its craftspeople (leatherworkers, potters, painters) and culinary artists, resulting in a plethora of restaurants and craft shops in the surrounding villages, making this a very interesting area in which to spend several days. I always head for the **Nicholas Mosse Pottery** in Bennetsbridge where you can purchase quality seconds, as well as watch skilled potters making and decorating this classic spongewear. (*Open all year, tel: 056 27105, fax: 056 27491, website: www.nicholasmosse.com.*)

The Southwest

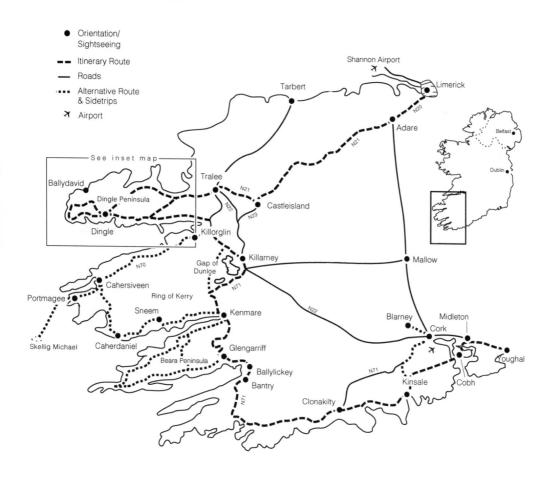

Orientation/ Sightseeing

Itinerary Route

Roads

Alternative Route & Sidetrips

Airport

Shannon Airport

Tarbert

Limerick

Belfast

Adare

Dublin

See inset map

Ballydavid

Tralee

N21

Dingle Peninsula

Castleisland

N22

N23

Dingle

Killorglin

Mallow

Killarney

Gap of Dunloe

N70

Cahersiveen

Ring of Kerry

N71

Portmagee

Sneem

Kenmare

Blarney

Midleton

Cork

N22

Skellig Michael

Caherdaniel

Beara Peninsula

Glengarriff

Youghal

Ballylickey

Bantry

N71

Kinsale

Cobh

N71

Clonakilty

The Southwest

The scenery of the southwest is absolutely magnificent: the mellow charm of Kinsale Harbor, the rugged landscape that winds you towards Glengarriff and its island filled with subtropical vegetation, the pretty 19th-century town of Kenmare, the translucent lakes of Killarney, and the ever-changing light on spectacular seascapes on the Dingle Peninsula. Relish the fabled beauties of this lovely part of Ireland. Take time to detour to Blarney to take part in the tradition of climbing atop Blarney Castle to kiss the stone that is said to confer "the gift of the gab." Do not hurry: allow time to linger over breakfast, enjoy a chat over a glass of Guinness, sample fresh salmon and scallops, and join in an evening singsong in a local pub.

Kinsale

The Southwest

Recommended Pacing: For this itinerary, select two places to stay near the coast, one in either Kenmare or Killarney, and one in Dingle. Allow one or two nights in each spot.

Your journey to the southwest begins in **Youghal** (pronounced "yawl"). Sir Walter Raleigh, who introduced the potato and tobacco from the New World, was once its mayor. It's a pleasant, old town dominated by the clock tower, which was built in 1776 and served as the town's jail. The one-way traffic system makes it impossible to explore without parking the car and walking. Several of the Main Street shops have been refurbished, but the town still has an unspoiled look to it. Make your first stop the **Heritage Centre** with its displays on the town, where you can pick up a brochure that outlines a walking tour of the old buildings.

Traveling the N25, a 30-kilometer drive brings you to the heart of **Midleton** where you find the **Jameson Heritage Centre** in the old whiskey distillery. Marvel at the world's largest pot distillery in the courtyard (capacity 143,872 liters), learn about whiskey production, visit the huge waterwheel, and be rewarded by a sample of the golden liquor. There's also a shop and café. (*Open Mar–Oct, tel: 021 4631821.*)

Nearby **Cobh** (pronounced "cove") was renamed Queenstown to mark the visit of Queen Victoria in 1849 and reverted back to Cobh in 1922. There's a long tradition of naval operations here, as its large harbor is a safe anchorage. The **Cobh Experience**, an audio-visual display housed in the restored Victorian railway station, tells the story of this port. Cobh was the point of departure for many emigrants off to seek a better life in America and Australia. For many it was the last piece of Irish soil they stood on before taking a boat to a new life. The ill-fated *Lusitania* was torpedoed not far from Cobh and survivors were brought here. It was also the last port of call of the *Titanic*. There's an excellent shop and café—an enjoyable place to spend a couple of hours on a rainy day. (*Open May–Sep.*)

Retrace your steps a short distance to the **Carriagaloe-Glenbrook ferry**, which transports you across Cork harbor and eliminates the hassle of driving through Cork city. A short, countryside drive brings you to **Kinsale**, its harbor full of tall-masted boats.

Narrow, winding streets are lined with quaint and several sadly derelict houses lead up from the harbor. Kinsale has some attractive shops and a great variety of restaurants. For lunch, Fishy Fishy is an excellent choice. At all but the ethnic restaurants, reservations are needed for dinner. It's a pleasant pastime to check the menus on display as you inhale mouth-watering aromas and peek at happy people enjoying their food. A good way to orient yourself is to take the walking tour which leaves the tourist office at 11:15 am.

There has been a fortress in Kinsale since Norman times. A great battle nearby in 1601 precipitated the flight of the earls and sounded the death knell of the ancient Gaelic civilization. It was from Kinsale that James II left for exile after his defeat at Boyne Water.

About 3 kilometers east of Kinsale, the impressive, 17th-century **Charles Fort** stands guard over the entrance to its harbor. It takes several hours to tour the five bastions that make up the complex. The ordnance sheds are restored and hold a photographic and historical exhibition about the fort. (*Open mid-Mar–Oct, tel: 021 4772263.*)

Across the estuary, you see the 1603 **James Fort** where William Penn's father was governor of Kinsale, while William worked as a clerk of the Admiralty Court. Later, William was given a land grant in America on which he founded the state of Pennsylvania.

SIDE TRIP TO BLARNEY

*About a half-hour drive north of Kinsale lie **Blarney Castle** and its famous tourist attraction, the **Blarney Stone**. Kissing the Blarney Stone, by climbing atop the keep and hanging upside-down, is said to confer the "gift of the gab." Even if you are not inclined to join in this backbreaking, unhygienic pursuit, the castle is worth a visit. (Open all year, tel: 021 4385252.) The gardens are beautiful, there's several well-signposted walks, the village is adorable with its shops round the village green, and there's a great shopping opportunity at **Blarney Woolen Mills** for allthings Irish, particularly knitwear.*

Blarney Castle

Leave Kinsale along the harbor, cross the River Bandon, and follow country lanes to the sleepy, little village of **Ballinspittle**. As you drive through the village, it is hard to imagine that in 1985 it was overwhelmed by pilgrims. They came to the village shrine after a local girl reported seeing the statue of the Virgin Mary rocking back and forth. You pass the shrine on your right just before you come to the village. Follow country lanes to **Timoleague**, a very small coastal village watched over by the ruins of a Franciscan abbey, and on to the N71 and **Clonakilty** and **Skibbereen**. As you travel westwards, rolling fields in every shade of green present themselves.

Arriving at the waterfront in **Bantry**, you come to **Bantry House**. Like so many other Irish country houses, it has seen better days, but the present owner, Egerton Shelswell-

White, makes visitors welcome and gives a typed information sheet—in the language of your choice—that guides you room-by-room through the house. The house has a wonderful collection of pictures, furniture, and works of art, brought together by the second Earl of Bantry during his European travels in the first half of the 19th century. In contrast to his ancestors' staid portraits, Egerton is shown playing his trombone. (*Open all year, tel: 027 50047.*)

Apart from furnishing the house, the second Earl, inspired by the gardens of Europe, laid out a formal Italian garden and a "staircase to the sky," the steep terraces rising up to the crest of the hill behind the house. If you are not up to the climb, you can still enjoy a magnificent, though less lofty view across the boat-filled bay from the terrace in front of the house. A very pleasant tea and gift shop occupies the old kitchen. One wing of the house has been renovated and modernized to provide upmarket bed & breakfast accommodation.

In the stable block next to the house, the **1796 Bantry French Armada Centre** relates the story of the French Armada's attempt to invade Ireland in 1796. It failed and a model of one of the armada's ships that sank in Bantry Bay is on display—a very interesting look at a little-known piece of Irish history. (*Open Apr–Oct, tel: 027 50047.*)

Eight kilometers north lies **Ballylickey**.

SIDE TRIP TO GOUGANE BARRA LAKE

*From Ballylickey an inland excursion takes you to **Gougane Barra Lake**, a beautiful lake locked into a ring of mountains. Here you find a small hotel where you can stop for a snack or a warming drink, and a little church on an island in the lake, the oratory where St. Finbarr went to contemplate and pray. The road to and from the lake takes you over a high pass and through mountain tunnels.*

Continue along the N71 and just before you enter **Glengarriff**, turn left for the harbor to take a ferryboat for the ten-minute ride to Garinish Island, a most worthwhile trip. (*Harbour Queen Ferryboats, tel: 027 63116, fax: 027 63298.*) **Garinish Island**, once a barren rock where only gorse and heather grew, was transformed into a miniature botanical paradise at the beginning of this century by a Scottish politician, Arran Bryce. The sheltered site of the island provides perfect growing conditions for trees, shrubs, and flowers from all over the world. It took a hundred men over three years to sculpt this lovely spot with its formal Italian garden, caseta, and temple. (*Open Apr–Oct, closed Sat, tel: 027 63081.*)

From Glengarriff, the road winds upwards and, glancing behind, you have a spectacular view of **Bantry Bay** lying beyond a patchwork of green fields. Rounding the summit, the road tunnels through a large buttress of rock and you emerge to stunning views of sparse, rocky hillsides.

Cross the River Kenmare into **Kenmare**. This delightful town of gray stone houses, with gaily painted shopfronts lining two broad main streets, is a favorite with tourists who prefer its peace and charm to the hectic pace of Killarney. Kenmare is full of excellent shops: **Cleo's** has outstanding knitwear, **Quills** has vast quantities of woolens, **Brenmar Jon** sells top-of-the-line fine knitwear, **The Craft Shop** offers souvenirs and pottery, and **Nostalgia** offers antique and new linen and lace. The town also has some delightful restaurants: **The Purple Heather**, a daytime bistro; **Packies**, a lively restaurant; the charming **Lime Tree** restaurant in the Old Schoolhouse; and **The Park Hotel** with its opulent afternoon silver-service teas and superb restaurant. Visit the **Heritage Centre** with its displays of locally made lace (*tel: 064 41233*). Just a short walk from the Heritage Centre, the **Kenmare Stone Circle** is the largest in the southwest of Ireland. Walks abound, from strolling along the broad river estuary to strenuous hill hikes. Kenmare is a perfect base for exploring both the Iveragh (Ring of Kerry) and Beara peninsulas and for visiting Killarney. It also serves as a stepping-off point for a side trip to Skellig Michael.

SIDE TRIP TO THE BEARA PENINSULA

*If you do not stop along the way, it will take you between two and three hours to drive the **Beara Peninsula**, where the scenery is wild, but gorgeous. From Kenmare, a minor road (R571) takes you along the north shore of the peninsula to **Ardgroom**, a picturesque village nestled beside a little harbor at the foot of the mountains. Farther west, **Eyeries** village looks out over the Skellig Rocks and several rocky inlets. Behind the village, the mountain road rises up through the Pass of Boffickle for a fantastic view back over the bay. In the 19th century, **Allihies** was a center of the copper mining industry, but now it is a resort with a magnificent beach curving along the bay. At the most westerly point of the peninsula lies **Garinish**, where a cable car takes visitors over to **Dursey Island**.*

Dursey is a long, mountain island encircled by high cliffs. Offshore are several other islands, the most interesting of which is Bull Rock, a roosting place for gannets. A cave passes right through it, creating a massive rock arch.

*Skirting the southern shore of the peninsula, the narrow road hugs the ocean through **Castletownbere** and **Adrigole**, from where you can follow the coastal road into Glengarriff or take the opportunity for a spectacular view by turning left and ascending the **Healy Pass**. It's hard to turn and admire the vista of **Bantry Bay** as the road gently zigzags up the pass, so stop at the top to relish the view before continuing down to **Lauraugh,** where you turn right for Kenmare.*

The Southwest

SIDE TRIP TO IVERAGH PENINSULA—RING OF KERRY

Instead of following the itinerary, you can use the Ring of Kerry as a route to Dingle or Killarney, or as a daytrip, traveling the complete "Ring" from Kenmare to Kenmare.

*The drive round the **Iveragh Peninsula** is, in my opinion, somewhat overrated, but if you want to see the much-publicized **Ring of Kerry**, hope that the fickle Irish weather is at its best. For when mists wreathe the Ring, it takes a lot of imagination to conjure up seascapes as you drive down fog-shrouded lanes. Even if the weather is dull, do not lose heart because at any moment the sun could break through. Driving the Ring can be a trial during the busy summer months when the roads are choked with tourist coaches, but your trip will be more enjoyable if you take advantage of some local knowledge before starting your journey. The coaches leave Killarney between 10 and 11 am and travel around the Ring in a counterclockwise direction, arriving back in Killarney by 5 pm. I prefer to meet the coaches head on (see below) rather than inhale their exhaust fumes and suggest an early start to meet them later in the day. If you prefer to avoid them totally: make an early start, travel counterclockwise, and make certain that you are beyond Killarney before 9:30 am.*

*Beginning the Ring, a pleasant drive takes you along the Kenmare river estuary and you get tempting glimpses of water and the Beara Peninsula. Arriving at **Sneem**, enjoy the most picturesque village on the Ring, with its tiny, gaily painted houses bordering two village greens. (The most beautiful coastal scenery lies between Sneem and Waterville.)*

*Continuing your journey westward you come to **Caherdaniel** village where you turn left for **Derrynane House**, the home of Daniel O'Connell, "The Liberator," a title he earned for winning Catholic emancipation. If the weather is inclement, concentrate on the house with its furnished rooms, audio-visual presentation, museum, and tearooms. But if the weather is fine, spend your time outdoors walking along the sandy beach of Derrynane Bay and crossing the narrow strip of sand that separates the mainland from **Abbey Island** where St. Fionan founded a monastic order over 1,000 years ago. Just round the point lies **Iskeroon** and **Bunavalla** pier where boats leave for the Skellig Islands (see*

"Side Trip to Skellig Michael"). A panoramic view of Derrynane Bay can be enjoyed form the Scariff Inn—you cannot miss the landmark bright-red pub sitting beside the road 3 kilometers above the seashore.

*Cresting the Coomakesta Pass, you turn north for **Waterville**, an aptly named town surrounded by water. Its main street with several colorfully painted houses is built along the shore. From here a pleasant drive takes you to **Cahersiveen,** a classic Irish town with a long main street made up of shops and pubs. Onwards you go to **Killorglin** and then to **Killarney** and back to **Kenmare** (see Kenmare to Killarney drive on next page). However, our suggested route for your return to Kenmare is to take a right-hand turn to **Caragh Lake** (5 kilometers before your reach Killorglin) and follow the narrow lanes around this beautiful lake and across the rugged **Macgillycuddy's Reeks** (Ireland's highest mountains) to Blackwater Bridge (on the Ring) and Kenmare—a trip to be undertaken only on a clear day.*

SIDE TRIP TO SKELLIG MICHAEL

Skellig Michael *is a very special place, a rocky island topped by the ruins of an ancient monastery lying 12 kilometers off the coast of the Ring of Kerry. Boats run daily between Easter and October, and you need to call at least two days in advance to make a reservation. However, the trip to the island cannot be counted upon until the actual day because it depends on calm seas. Boat service operates from several harbors on the Ring of Kerry—Bunavalla: Kenneth Roddy, www.skelligtrips.com, email: ken@skelligtrips.com; Seamus Shea, tel: 066 9475129; Portmagee: Des Lavelle, tel: 066 9476124, email: lavelles@indigo.ie; or Brendan O'Keefe, Fisherman's Bar, tel: 066 9477103. Remember to wear flat-heeled shoes and take a waterproof jacket, an extra sweater, and lunch. The morning departure for the island and the late afternoon return necessitate your spending two nights on the Ring of Kerry (see listings in Caherdaniel, Caragh Lake, and Kenmare).*

View to Little Skellig from Skellig Michael

After you arrive at the cove beneath the looming rock, the first part of your ascent follows the path to the abandoned lighthouse, past seabirds' nests clinging to tiny crevasses in the steep rock slopes. As you round a corner, the monks' stairway appears and you climb up hundreds and hundreds of hand-hewn stone steps to the monastery perched on a ledge, high above the pounding ocean. Pausing to catch your breath, you marvel at the monks who set out in fragile, little boats to establish this monastery and toiled with crude implements to build these steps up the sheer rock face.

At the summit, six little beehive huts, a slightly larger stone oratory, and the roofless walls of a small church nestle against the hillside, some poised at the edge—only a low stone wall between them and the churning ocean far below. *The windowless interiors of the huts hardly seem large enough for a person to lie down. Remarkably, the monks' only water source was rainwater runoff stored in rock fissures. The Office of Public Works is maintaining and restoring the site and there might be someone there to impart information.*

It is reputed that the monks arrived in 600 A.D. According to annals, the Vikings raided in 812 and 823 and found an established community. It is documented that the last monks departed in the 13th century. When it is time to leave this spot, you feel a sense of wonder for the men who toiled in this rocky place, enduring deprivation, hardship, and solitude to achieve a state of grace.

As a complement (or alternative) to visiting Skellig Michael, visit the **Skellig Heritage Centre** *on Valencia Island. The center is found where the road bridge meets the island, directly opposite Portmagee. An audio-visual presentation, "The Call of the Skelligs," takes you to the Skellig Michael monastery while displays show the bird and sea life of the islands. (Open Apr–mid-Nov, tel: 066 9476306.)*

From Kenmare travel over one of Ireland's most beautiful roads (N71) for the twisty 34-kilometer drive over mountains to Killarney, stopping at **Ladies' View** to admire a spectacular panorama with the lakes of Killarney spread at your feet.

In amongst the woodlands you find the car park for **Torc Waterfall**. Following the stream, a short uphill walk brings you to the celebrated 20-meter cascade of water.

Muckross House and Gardens are 5 kilometers out of Killarney on the Kenmare road. (Be sure to choose the entrance gate that enables you to take your car to the car park beside the house). Tudor-style Muckross was built in 1843 in an enviable position beside the lake. The main rooms are furnished in splendid Victorian style and the remainder of the house serves as a folk museum with various exhibits. There's also a bustling gift shop and tearoom. (*Open daily, Mar–Nov, tel: 064 31440, fax: 064 33926.*) The gardens surrounding the house are lovely, containing many subtropical plants, and there is no more delightful way to tour the grounds than by horse and trap. Take a step back in time and visit **Muckross Traditional Farms** (the entrance is on the opposite side of the car park to the house). Stroll up the lane (or ride the old bus) to visit three farms that demonstrate what Kerry farming was like in the 1930s before the advent of electricity and farming machinery. Chat with the farmers and their wives as they go about their daily work. Muckross House and its vast estate were given to the Irish nation by the Bourne family of California, who had a smaller, lakeside estate, Filoli, just south of San Francisco.

Believe everything you ever read about the magnificent beauty of the Killarney lakes, but realize that **Killarney**, not an attractive town, is absolutely packed with tourists during the summer season. If you would like additional views of the lakes, then a tour to Aghadoe Hill or a boat trip from Ross Castle should give you what you are looking for. Leave Killarney on the road to Tralee (N22) and turn left for the 5-kilometer drive to **Aghadoe**, where Killarney town, lakes, and mountains can all be seen from this vantage point. If you prefer a close look at the lake and its island, take the 90-minute boat tour of the lower lake, which leaves from the jetty alongside Ross Castle. Tickets for this trip can be purchased from the tourist office in town. **Ross Castle** has been restored and you can climb its steep, stone stairs to see what living in a castle was like.

SIDE TRIP UP THE GAP OF DUNLOE

*The road through the **Gap of Dunloe** (signposted from the Killorglin road just past the golf course) is a single-lane dirt track up a 6-kilometer ravine carved by glaciers. **Kate Kearney's Cottage** sits at the entrance to the ravine. Legend has it that Kate was a beautiful witch who drove men wild with desire—now her home is greatly enlarged as a coffee and souvenir shop. As you travel up the gap the dramatic setting is enhanced by the purple mountains on your left and **Macgillycuddy's Reeks** on your right.*

In the past I have recommended an evening drive up the gap to emerge on the N71, just west of Moll's Gap, and returning to Killarney with a quick stop at Ladies' View to admire the unparalleled views of the lakes of Killarney. Signs have been posted to discourage motor traffic. I recommend that you either park your car near Kate Kearney's cottage and walk, arrange for a jaunting car to take you up the gap or purchase a ticket at the tourist office for the Dero Tours day trip. This includes a shuttle service from your lodging to the gap, horse or jaunting car rides up the ravine, transportation by electric boat through the lakes of Killarney, and transportation back to your lodging.

Ladies' View, Killarney

The Dingle Peninsula

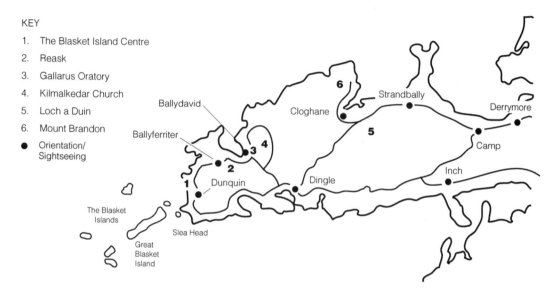

KEY

1. The Blasket Island Centre
2. Reask
3. Gallarus Oratory
4. Kilmalkedar Church
5. Loch a Duin
6. Mount Brandon
● Orientation/ Sightseeing

Leaving Killarney, a two-hour drive will bring you to Limerick, but rather than taking a direct route, take the time to explore the lovely **Dingle Peninsula**. It's a very special place, a narrow promontory of harshly beautiful land and seascapes where the people are especially friendly and welcoming to strangers. The road from Killarney to Dingle town takes you northwest to **Castlemaine** where you follow the coast road west through **Inch** to Dingle town, the largest settlement on the peninsula (it's only an hour-and-a-half drive from Killarney to Dingle).

Colorfully painted pubs, shops, and houses welcome you to **Dingle** (*An Daingean*) where fishing boats bob in the harbor unloading bountiful catches of fish and shellfish. It is not surprising that you find a great many excellent seafood restaurants here: **The Half Door** and adjacent **Doyle's** are two upmarket favorites. After dinner, ask where you can go to hear traditional Irish music. Dingle's population is under 2,000, yet it has over 50 pubs, some of which double as shops—like **Foxy John's**, where you can buy hardware while enjoying a drink, and **McCarthy's** with its poetry readings. There are several interesting shops—**Brian de Staic's** jewelry store contains exquisite gold and silver jewelry inspired by Dingle's flora and ancient Celtic motifs. The town's most famous resident is **Fungie**, a playful, bottle-nosed dolphin who took up residence in the harbor in 1985 and who loves to perform for visitors (tour boats leave from the harbor).

Plan to spend at least two nights on the peninsula to experience the beauty and tranquility offered by the unspoiled scenery of the spectacular beaches and rocky promontories that lie to the west of Dingle town. Take time to wander along the beaches or walk along the lanes, where fuchsia hedges divide the fields and friendly locals wave a salute of welcome, and to take the trip to the Blasket Islands. Because Irish is the official language of the peninsula, signposts are in Irish (though commercial maps are in English) so we give the Irish in parentheses to aid you in finding your way. We outline a route that will take you on a half-day drive around Slea Head. But for a real appreciation of the 2,000 archaeological sites of the Dingle Peninsula (peppered with lots of interesting stories), we recommend forsaking your car and taking one of **Sciuird's** minivan or walking tours. Michael and his dad, Timothy, offer tours that range from an hour's walk round Dingle town to visiting ancient, Ogham stones, wedge tombs, standing stones, and ring forts. (*Sciuird, Holyground, Dingle, Co Kerry, tel: 066 9151606, email: collinskirrary@eircom.net.*)

The road to Slea Head, signposted as **Slea Head Drive** (*Ceann Sléibhe*), twists and turns, following the contours of the increasingly rocky coast. Stunning seascapes present themselves, demanding that you pause just to admire the view. Several of the farms along the way have beehive stone huts and, for a small fee, the farmers will let you climb up to visit them. Conjecture has it that these small huts were used by early pilgrims traveling the St. Brendan's pilgrimage route. A large, white crucifix marks **Slea Head**, which affords the first view of the **Blasket Islands** (*Na Blascaodaí*), alternately sparkling like jewels in the blue ocean and disappearing under dark clouds a moment later.

Around the point, the scattered village of **Dunquin** (*Dún Chaoin*) and the **Blasket Island Centre** come into view. The building is impressive, with exhibits lining a long corridor that leads to an observatory overlooking the island's abandoned village. Remarkably, this tiny, isolated island abode produced an outpouring of music and writing. Three classics of Irish literature emerged with Peig Sayers' *Peig,* Thomas Crohan's *The Islandman*, and Maurice O'Sullivan's *Twenty Years a'Growing*. The islands have been uninhabited since 1953, when the last islanders evacuated their windswept homes. The center's large, airy dining room serves food and provides enticing island views. (*Open all year, tel: 066 9156444.*)

Before you visit the center, take a left turn, park on the cliff top (opposite the two yellow bungalows), and walk down to Dunquin's **pier**, which sits away from the scattered village and is reached by a steep path that zigzags down the cliff. As you round the last twist, you see curraghs turned upside-down looking like giant, black beetles stranded high above the water line. Curraghs are fragile boats made of tarred canvas stretched over a wooden skeleton. St. Brendan is reputed to have discovered America in such a boat. In clear weather a ferry takes day-trip visitors to and from **Great Blasket Island**. The little village on the island is mostly in ruins, and paths wander amongst the fields where the hardy islanders struggled to earn a living—a café offers the only shelter. (*Ferry sails every hour 10 am–6 pm in summer, tel: 066 9156444.*)

On the road to **Ballyferriter** (*Balle an Fheirtearaigh*), the pottery of **Louis Mulcahy** makes an interesting stop. During the summer you can try your hand at throwing a pot, and thus gain an appreciation for how difficult it is. (*Open all year 10 am–5:30 pm.*) One kilometer after driving through **Ballyferriter** (*Balle an Fheirtearaigh*), an attractive little village with a couple of pubs, pass Tig Bhric (a pub and shop) on your right and make a right-hand turn (small signpost) to **Reask** (*Riasc*), an ancient monastic settlement with its large slab cross and foundations of beehive huts.

Returning to the main road, a couple of kilometers' drive brings you to the **Gallarus Oratory** (*Séipéilín Ghallarais*). Over 1,000 years ago many of St. Brendan's contemporaries lived on the Dingle Peninsula in unmortared, beehive-shaped stone huts called clochans. The most famous example is the Gallarus Oratory, a tiny church built not as a circle, but in the shape of an upturned boat. It has a small window at one end, a small door at the other, and is as watertight today as when it was built over 900 years ago. A privately run enterprise offers a little visitors' center and a café, and charges a fee to cross their land to visit the monument. If you would rather not pay a fee, drive up the adjacent, public road and the monument is signed a short walk to your left.

Arriving in the nearby village of **Múirioch,** turn right at the Y for **Kilmalkedar Church** (*Séipéal Chill Mhaolcéadair*). This now-roofless place of worship was built in the 12th century on the site of a 7th-century church. However, it dates back even further, for within the graveyard is a magnificent, early Christian cross, an ancient Ogham stone, and an intricately decorated sundial. Within the church stands a rare alphabet stone, which the monks used for teaching the alphabet. Locals refer to the little slit east window as the eye of the needle and folklore has it that if you climb through the window, you will surely marry within a year and a day.

Continuing uphill, the field to your right contains the ruins of the Chancellor's House. Park your car by the gate on the right that follows the little lane (not signposted) and walk into the farmer's field to examine the waist-high foundations of the **Caher Dorgan** (*Cathar Dairgáin*) ring fort with its beehive huts. On a clear day, you get a magnificent view of the Three Sisters, a line of three mountains that tumble into the sea.

Cresting the rise, you travel 5 kilometers of the Dingle Peninsula's straightest road, known as *An Bóthar Fada*—The Long Road. It must have seemed a very long road for farmers walking to town. In the distance, the entrance to Dingle's harbor is guarded by **Esk Tower**, built in 1847 by an English landlord to give paid work to the men of Dingle. Its giant wooden hand serves as a marker for fishermen to the entrance to the protected harbor.

NOTE: If you get lost on the peninsula's little lanes, ask a friendly local or follow signposts for *An Daingean*, Dingle town.

There are lots of interesting walks on the Dingle Peninsula. Two of the more unusual ones are following the **Way of St. Brendan**, and exploring the **Loch a Duin Valley**. The Way of St. Brendan is laid out on a map that you obtain at **Cloghane's** tiny tourist office. The route begins in nearby Brandon and follows a well-marked route that the saint supposedly took to the top of **Mount Brandon** (about five hours of walking). Cloghane's tourist office also sells a booklet that takes you on a self-guided tour through the Loch a Duin Valley (Sciuird also leads a walking tour). Beginning at the hut beside the road at the bottom of Connor Pass, this route leads you on a well-marked, three-hour walk through the valley's boglands. Structures associated with prehistoric habitation (2,000 B.C.), ritual, and agriculture, along with several kilometers of prehistoric field wall, still survive. The valley is also of interest to bird watchers, botanists, and geologists.

Leaving the Dingle Peninsula (signposted Tralee), the **Connor Pass** twists you upward to the summit, where a backward glance gives you a magnificent view of Dingle and its harbor. The view is spectacular, but there is no guarantee that you will see it—all will be green fields, blue sea and sky, until the mists roll in and everything vanishes. Follow the coast road through **Ballyduff**, **Stradbally**, and **Camp** to **Tralee**. (If you are heading for the Cliffs of Moher, take the N69 to the **Tarbert ferry**, which takes you across the River Shannon.) At Tralee you join the main road (N21) for the drive to **Castleisland** and on to **Adare** with its charming row of thatched cottages and tree-lined streets. Less than an hour's drive will find you in **Limerick**, whose traffic-crowded streets can be avoided by taking the ring road signposted Ennis and Shannon Airport.

Dingle

The West

Céide Fields

Sligo

Bangor

N59

N59

Crossmolina   Ballina

Achill Island   Lough Conn   N17

Mulrany

Newport

Rosturk   N59   Castlebar

Louisburgh   Westport

Inishbofin   N59
Island

Leenane

Lough Mask

Cleggan

Letterfrack

Clifden   Lough Corrib

Oughterard   Aughnanure Castle

Roundstone

Rossaveel   Galway

Dunguaire
Castle

Aran Islands

Kilronan   Thoor
Ballylee

Dún Aengus

Lisdoonvarna   Ballyvaughan

The
Burren   Kilfenora

Corofin   N18

Ennis

Shannon Airport

Limerick

Belfast

Dublin

● Orientation/
  Sightseeing

━ ━ Itinerary Route

── Roads

••• Alternative Route
    & Sidetrips

✈ Airport

57

The West

This itinerary takes you off the beaten tourist track through the wild, hauntingly beautiful scenery of Connemara, and County Mayo. Lying on the coast of County Clare, The Burren presents a vast landscape of smooth, limestone rocks—whose crevices are ablaze with rock roses, blue gentians, and all manner of Arctic and Alpine flowers in the spring and early summer. Otherwise, there are no trees, shrubs, rivers, or lakes—just bare "moonscapes" of rocks dotted with forts and ruined castles, tombs, and rock cairns. Traveling to Connemara, your route traces the vast, island-dotted Lough Corrib and traverses boglands and moorlands. Distant mountains fill the horizon and guide you to the coast, where gentle waves lap at rocky inlets sheltering scattered villages with whitewashed cottages dotting the landscape. Ireland's holy mountain, Croagh Patrick, and the windswept Achill Island leave a deep impression on the visitor.

Cliffs of Moher

Recommended Pacing: It is possible to tour the west in just a few days, but this beautiful area calls for you to linger. Our ideal would be one or two nights on or near The Burren, two or three nights in Connemara, and two or three nights near either Crossmolina or Sligo.

Leave **Limerick** in the direction of Ennis and Shannon airport and you soon arrive at **Bunratty Castle and Folk Park**. An interesting history and guide to the castle is available at the entrance. As the majority of castles in Ireland stand roofless and in ruins, it is a treat to visit a 15th-century castle that has been restored so beautifully. The authentic 14th- to 17th-century furniture in the rooms gives the castle a real lived-in feel. In the evenings, firelit banquets warmed with goblets of mead whisk visitors back to the days when the castle was young. In the castle grounds, a folk park contains several cottages, farmhouses, and a whole 19th-century village street of shops, houses, and buildings furnished appropriately for their era. The community is brought to life by costumed townspeople who bake, make butter, and tend the animals. (*Open daily, tel: 061 360788, fax: 061 472523.*) **Bunratty Cottage**, opposite the castle, offers a wide range of handmade Irish goods, and just at the entrance to the park is **Durty Nelly's**, one of Ireland's most popular pubs, dating from the 1600s.

Just to the northwest lies the strangest landscape in Ireland, **The Burren**. Burren means "a rocky place" and this is certainly the case for, as far as the eye can see, this is a wilderness—a wilderness that is rich in archaeological sites (megalithic tombs, ring forts, and the remains of ancient huts) and strange rock formations whose tiny crevices are a mass of Arctic, Mediterranean, and Alpine flowers in springtime. Ludlow, one of Cromwell's generals, passing through the area in 1649, wrote, "There is not enough wood to hang a man, nor water to drown him, nor earth enough to bury him in."

Base yourself at either **Corofin** or **Ballyvaughan** (see *Places to Stay*) to explore this unique area. One of the most photographed sights, the **Poulnabrone Portal Tomb,** is found alongside the road between Corofin and Ballyvaughan.

To help you appreciate this unusual landscape, first visit The **Burren Display Centre** at **Kilfenora**, which offers a film on the geology and rare flora and fauna of the area. Models explain the pattern of settlement and the geological makeup of the area, and show the non-botanist what to look for. Next to the Centre, the crumbling remains of Ladies Chapel has a glass roof sheltering three celtic crosses with symbolic carvings from the elements. A fourth cross is open to the elements in an adjacent field.

Turn right as you leave the interpretive center and left as you come to the main road to reach the **Cliffs of Moher**—the most spectacular section of the coastline—where towering cliffs rise above the pounding Atlantic Ocean. These majestic cliffs, stretching along 5 kilometers of the coast, are one of Ireland's most popular sights. The cliffs face due west, which means that the best time to see them is on a bright, summer evening. The visitors' center offers welcome shelter on cool and windy days. A short distance from the visitors' center, **O'Brien's Tower** (built in 1835 by Sir Cornelius O'Brien, Member of Parliament, for "strangers visiting the magnificent scenery of this neighborhood") marks the highest and most photographed point along the clifftops.

On leaving the cliffs, head north toward, but not into, Lisdoonvarna. Follow the coastal road around Black Head, where the rocky Burren spills into Galway Bay—to Ballyvaughan, where you turn right following signs for the **Aillwee Caves** on the bluff above. The visitors' center is so cleverly designed that it is hard to distinguish it from the surrounding gray landscape. Beneath the eerie "moonscape" of the Burren lie vast caves, streams, and lakes. You can take a tour through a small section of these underground caverns. The first is called Bear Haven because the bones of a brown bear that died long ago were found here. In other chambers, you see limestone cascades, stalactites, and stalagmites before the tour ends at the edge of an underground river. Remember to dress warmly, for it's cool in the caves. (*Open all year, www.aillweecave.ie, tel: 065 7077036.*)

Retrace your steps a short distance down the road towards Ballyvaughan and take the first turn left, passing Gregans Castle hotel and up Corkscrew Hill, a winding road that takes you from a lush, green valley to the gray, rocky landscape above. Take the first turn to the left and you come to **Cahermacnaghten**, a ring fort that was occupied until the 18th century. You enter via a medieval two-story gateway, and the foundations of buildings of similar date can be seen inside the stone wall.

Some 7 kilometers farther south, you come to another ring fort, **Ballykinvarga**. You have to walk several hundred meters before you see the Iron-Age fort surrounded by its defensive, pointed stones known as *chevaux de frise*, a term derived from a military expression describing how Dutch Frisians used spikes to impede attackers. Ireland has three other such forts, of which the two most impressive are found on the Aran Islands.

When you leave The Burren, head directly for the coast and follow it east (N67) to **Kinvarra**, a pretty village with boats bobbing in the harbor and small rocky islands separating it from the expanse of Galway Bay. On the outskirts of the village, the restored **Dunguaire Castle** has a craft shop and, on summer evenings, hosts medieval banquets. (*Open May–Oct, tel: 091 637108.*)

From the castle car park, turn towards the village and immediately take a left-hand turn (opposite the castle entrance) for the 5-kilometer drive to **Ardrahan**, where you turn right on the N18 and, after 6 kilometers, left for the 2-kilometer drive to **Thoor Ballylee**. William Butler Yeats bought this 13th-century tower house and cottage in 1917 and it was his summer home for 11 years. The cozy, thatched cottage is now a bookshop. An audio-visual presentation tells of Yeats's artistic and political achievements. Two floors of the tower are sparsely furnished as they were in his occupancy. By pressing a green button on each room's wall you receive information and hear excerpts of his poetry. (*Open May–Sep, tel: 091 631436.*) Leaving Thoor Ballylee, retrace your steps to the N18 for a 24-kilometer drive to **Galway**.

SIDE TRIP TO THE ARAN ISLANDS

*If you are planning to visit the **Aran Islands**, take the coastal route through Spiddal to **Rossaveel** where two ferry companies operate a shuttle service to **Kilronan** on **Inishmore**, the largest of the three Aran Islands. (Island Ferries, tel: 091 561767 and*

*091 568903.) Until a decade or so ago, time had stood still here and the way of life and the culture of the islanders had changed little. Now their traditional dress comes out only for TV cameras and special occasions, and their traditional way of life has been replaced by a more profitable one—tourism. In the summertime, more than double the population of the islands arrives on Inishmore as day-trippers. When you arrive, visit the Tourist Information Centre by the harbor to discuss the cost of horse and trap, bicycle (there are plenty of shops where you can rent bikes), and minibus transportation. The barren landscape is closely related to that of The Burren: sheer cliffs plunge into the pounding Atlantic Ocean along the southern coast, while the north coast flattens out with shallow, rock-ringed, sandy beaches. You will have no difficulty obtaining transportation to **Dún Aengus** (about 8 kilometers from the harbor), the best known of the island's stone forts, believed to date from the early Celtic period some two to three thousand years ago. It has sheer cliffs at its back and is surrounded by pointed boulders designed to twist ankles and skin shins. Despite the hordes of visitors scrambling over its walls and stones, Dún Aengus is remarkably well preserved. With four stone forts, remains of stone huts, high crosses, and ruined churches to examine, the archaeologically minded could spend many days with detailed map in hand exploring the islands.*

Those who are not island bound should follow signs for Clifden (N59) around Galway. Leaving the town behind, the road is straight and well paved, but a tad bouncy if you try to go too fast. Accommodation signs for nearby Oughterard alert you to watch for a right-hand turn to **Aughnanure Castle**. Approaching the castle, you may be greeted, as we were, by a friendly family of goats snoozing on the wooden footbridge before the castle gates. Aughnanure Castle was the stronghold of the ferocious O'Flahertys, who launched attacks on Galway town until their castle was destroyed by English forces in 1572. The clan regained their castle for a period of time until wars with Cromwell and William of Orange saw them expelled again. (*Open Jun–Sep, tel: 091 552214.*) Nearby **Oughterard** is a pleasant, bustling town, "the gateway to Connemara," whose main street has several, attractive shops. A stay here affords the opportunity for fishing and exploring the island-dotted Lough Corrib by boat.

Clifden

Beyond Oughterard, you plunge into Connemara past the **Twelve Bens** mountains, which dominate the wild, almost treeless landscape of bogs, lakes, and rivers; a landscape that is ever being changed by the dashing clouds that rush in from the Atlantic. Apart from the occasional craft shop, there are no houses until you reach **Clifden** (see listings) on the Atlantic coast (N59, 80 kilometers). Clifden is the major market town of Connemara and the home of the annual Connemara Pony Show (*third week in August*). The town presents a gay face with shopfronts painted in bright hues of red, blue, yellow, and green. Craft and tourist shops alternate with the butchers, the hardware store, pubs, and restaurants. On Market Street, you find the **Connemara Walking Centre** where you can buy booklets on the locale and sign up for one of the walking tours that vary from an interesting stroll through the Roundstone bogs—great walking amongst lakes full of otters and interesting plant life—to the demanding climb up one half of the great

Glanhoaghan Horseshoe in the stark Twelve Bens mountains. (*Contact Michael Gibbons, Connemara Walking Centre, Island House, Market Street, Clifden, Co Galway, tel: 095 21379, fax: 095 21845, email: walkwest@indigo.ie, website: www.walkingireland.com.*)

SIDE TRIP TO ROUNDSTONE

*To the south of Clifden, the road has more views of sea than land, as little boats bob in rocky inlets and cottages gaze westward across tiny islands. The road passes the marshy area where Alcock and Brown crash-landed after the first transatlantic flight in 1919 (commemorated by a monument about 500 meters from the main road). Via **Ballinaboy**, **Ballyconneely**, and **Roundstone**, the sweeping seascapes that this route presents are so compelling that it is difficult to concentrate on the driving.*

SIDE TRIP TO INISHBOFIN ISLAND

*If the weather is fine, a delightful day trip can be taken to **Inishbofin Island**. The Inishbofin boat leaves from Cleggan pier at 11:30 am, returning at 5 pm (the crossing takes less than an hour). Be at **Cleggan** pier half an hour before sailing time and buy your ticket at the Pier Bar. Sailings depend on weather conditions, so it's best to phone ahead to verify departure times. (Kings Ferries, Cleggan, tel: 095 21520 or The Inishbofin Experience, the O'Halloran family, tel: 095 45903/45806/45831.) The boat sails into the sheltered harbor presided over by the remains of a Cromwellian castle, and you wade ashore at a cluster of houses that make up the island's main settlement. Many islanders have left in search of greener pastures and their cottages have fallen into disrepair, but those who remain eke out a hard living from the land and the sea. As you walk down lanes edged with wild fuchsias and brightly colored wildflowers, whitewashed farmhouses appear and you see fields dotted with handmade haystacks. (Regrettably, the odd, long-abandoned, rusting car spoils the scene.) At the far side of the island, a row of cottages fronts the beach, one of them housing a welcoming little café, where you can have lunch or tea before walking back to the harbor to take the evening boat back to Cleggan.*

Clifden stands just outside the **Connemara National Park**, which covers 5,000 acres of mountain, heath, and bog—there are no pretty gardens or verdant woodlands. The video in the visitors' center gives a beautiful introduction to the park, which has wonderful hiking trails. If you want to tackle the smaller paths leading into the Twelve Bens mountains, consider joining one of the guided walks that begin at the visitors' center (four of the Twelve Bens, including Benbaum, the highest, are found in the park). Two signposted nature trails start at the center: one leads you through Ellis Wood while the other takes you into rougher terrain. (*Open Apr–Sep.*)

Leaving Clifden to the north, the N59 passes the much-photographed **Kylemore Abbey**. Originally built by a wealthy Englishman in the 19th century, this grand home, surrounded by greenery and fronting a lake, passed into the hands of Benedictine nuns who have a school here. You'll find ample parking (lots of coaches) and a large restaurant and gift shop. You can walk beside the lake to the abbey, where in summer the library is open to visitors. In the grounds, you can visit the restored Gothic chapel with its pretty, sandstone interior and different-colored, marble pillars. (*Open all year, tel: 095 41146.*) Follow the shore of **Killary Harbor**, the longest and most picturesque fjord in Ireland, to **Leenane**, a little village nestled at the head of the inlet. Continue along the shoreline and take the first turn to the left, signposted as a scenic route to Westport via Louisburgh. This interesting side road gently winds you along the sea lough to **Delphi**, an area of pools and loughs amongst some of the highest and wildest mountains in the west. Acres of woodlands offer shelter and there is not a bungalow in sight. The Marquis of Sligo built a lodge here in 1840 and called it "Delphi" because it reminded him of Delphi in Greece. After falling into dereliction, the house and estate were bought by the Mantles, who welcome guests to their restored home (see listing under Leenane).

Leaving Delphi, the isolated mountain road takes you along the shore of **Doo Lough** at the foot of **Mweelrea Mountain** and on through wild, remote scenery to **Louisburgh**; where, turning towards Westport, the summit of the conical-shaped **Croagh Patrick** (Ireland's most famous mountain) comes into view. Swirling mists substantiate its mystical place in Irish history. It was after St. Patrick spent the 40 days of Lent atop its rocky summit in 441 that the mountain became sacred to Christians. Every year thousands of penitential pilgrims begin their climb to the oratory at the summit at dawn on the last Sunday in July, several going barefoot up the stony track. The ritual involves stopping at three stations and reciting prayers. No climbing skills are needed as it's a well-worn path to the top and, on a clear day, a walk to the summit affords a panoramic view across Clew Bay to Achill Island.

Nearby **Westport** lies on the shore of Clew Bay and is unique amongst Irish towns because it was built following a pre-designed plan. The architect walled the river and lined the riverside malls with lime trees and austere Georgian homes, forming a most delightful thoroughfare. There's a buzz to the town and, on a sunny day, you can enjoy a drink at the tables and chairs outside **Geraghtey's Bar** and **Grand Central**, on the Octagon (the heart of the town with a granite pillar in the center of the square). At **Clew Bay Heritage Centre** on Westport Quay, postcards and old photographs show the town as it was at the turn of the last century. There is also a genealogical research center and a display on the maritime traditions of Westport. (*Open May–Sep, tel: 098 26852.*)

From Westport, the most direct route to Sligo is by way of the broad, well-paved, fast N5, and N17. However, if the weather is clear and bright, it is a delightful drive from Westport to Sligo via **Newport**, **Achill Island**, **Crossmolina**, and **Ballina**.

Achill Island is Ireland's largest offshore island. Traditionally, the Achill islanders traveled to Scotland as migrant farmworkers during the summer; but now the population that has not been enticed away by emigration, remains to garner a meager living from a harsh land. This was the home of the infamous British Captain Boycott; who gave his name to the English language when tenants "boycotted" him for his excessive rents during the potato famine. Today, this island holds the allure that belongs to wild and lonely places: in sunshine it is glorious; but in torrential rain, it is a grim and depressing place. On the island, take the first turn to your left, signposted for the windswept **Atlantic Drive**, where you drive along the tops of rugged cliffs carved by the pounding

Atlantic Ocean far below. The "drive" ends at **Knockmore** where scattered houses shelter from the biting winds.

Returning to Mulrany, turn north on the N59 for the 32-kilometer drive across boglands, where vast quantities of turf are harvested by mechanical means, to **Bangor** and on to **Crossmolina, Ballina,** and **Sligo**. The many sightseeing opportunities in the Sligo area are outlined in the following itinerary.

Croagh Patrick

SIDE TRIP TO CÉIDE FIELDS

*From Ballina, you can detour north 20 kilometers to Ballycastle and drive another 8 kilometers east to the great cliffs of **Downpatrick Head**, where the Stone-Age settlements at **Céide Fields** (pronounced "kay-jeh") are being excavated. Under the peat has been unearthed the most extensive Stone-Age settlement in the world, with walls older than the pyramids, a vast site which once supported a community of over 10,000 people. Wander* *round a portion of the archaeological dig, and enjoy an audio-visual presentation and a cup of tea in the pyramid-shaped visitors' center. (Open mid-Mar–Nov, tel: 096 43325.) The surrounding cliffs are amongst the most magnificent you will see in Ireland. Retrace your steps to Ballycastle, and take the R314 through **Killala** (a workaday village whose skyline is punctuated by an ancient, round tower) to **Ballina** where you turn left for **Sligo**.*

From the Sligo area—you can go into Northern Ireland, continue north on the following itinerary, or return south. If you travel south, consider visiting either **Ballintubber Abbey**, a beautifully restored church dating back to 1216, or the village of **Knock**. A religious apparition seen on the gable of the village church in 1879, and some hearty promotion, has led to the development of Knock as a religious pilgrimage site and a tourist venue. A giant basilica stands next to the little church, a large complex of religious souvenir shops sits across the road, and nearby Knock airport has a runway capable of providing landing facilities for large jets. Surrounded as it is by narrow country lanes, this sophisticated complex seems very out of place in rural Ireland.

The North

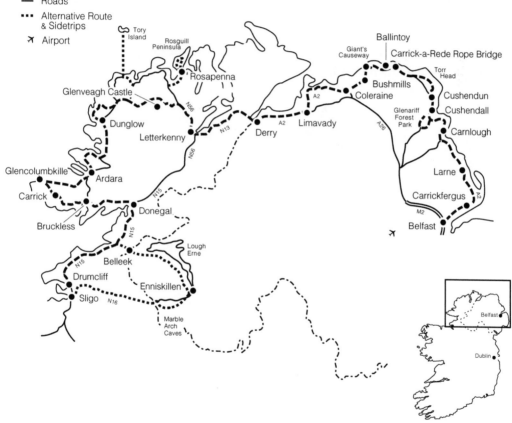

- ● Orientation/ Sightseeing
- ▪▪ Itinerary Route
- — Roads
- ▪▪▪ Alternative Route & Sidetrips
- ✈ Airport

Tory Island
Rosguill Peninsula
Rosapenna
Glenveagh Castle
Dunglow
Letterkenny
Derry
Limavady

Ballintoy
Carrick-a-Rede Rope Bridge
Giant's Causeway
Bushmills
Coleraine
Torr Head
Cushendun
Cushendall
Glenariff Forest Park
Carnlough

Glencolumbkille
Ardara
Carrick
Bruckless
Donegal

Larne
Carrickfergus
Belfast

Belleek
Lough Erne
Drumcliff
Enniskillen
Sligo
Marble Arch Caves

N56
N13
N56
N15
N15
N15
N16
A2
A2
A26
A2
M2

Belfast

Dublin

The North

The northernmost reaches of Ireland hold special appeal. Herein lies the countryside that inspired the moving poetry of William Butler Yeats. Beyond Donegal, narrow roads twist and turn around the wild, rugged coastline of County Donegal, where villagers weave their tweeds and Irish is often the spoken language and that written on the signposts. The Folk Village Museum at Glencolumbkille, with its authentically furnished, thatch-topped cottages, demonstrates the harsh living conditions of the far north. Crossing into Northern Ireland, the honeycomb columns of the Giant's Causeway signpost the Antrim coast full of cliffs, lush green headlands, and beautiful views.

Dunluce Castle

Recommended Pacing: Two or three nights around Sligo and Donegal, a night near Glenveagh National Park (to permit a leisurely visit), and two nights along the Antrim coast will give you time to explore this lovely area.

The county and town of **Sligo** are ever mindful of William Butler Yeats, and the whole area is promoted as being Yeats country. If you are an ardent admirer of the poet, you will want to visit the **County Museum**, which has a special section about his poetry and writing. Base yourself near the town for several days—**Ballymote** and **Riverstown** are our accommodation choices in the *Places to Stay* section. The countryside is very pretty and there is enough sightseeing to keep you busy for a week.

SIDE TRIP TO CARROWMORE AND CARROWKEEL

*Seven kilometers to the southwest of Sligo town, sitting in fields on either side of a narrow country lane, are the megalithic tombs of **Carrowmore**. Wander amongst the cows and explore the little stone circles and larger dolmens which make up what is reputed to be the largest Bronze-Age cemetery in Europe. Farther inland take the Boyle road (N4) 30 kilometers south of Sligo to Castlebaldwin, where you turn right following signposts for Carrowkeel. At the end of a mountain track, you come to **Carrowkeel**, a 4,000-year-old passage tomb cemetery. There are 13 cairns covering passage tombs, while the 14th is a long cairn. One of the tombs can be entered (backwards) and it is claimed that, on the summer solstice, the setting sun lights up the main chamber.*

SIDE TRIP AROUND LOUGH GILL

*A half-day sightseeing trip from Sligo can be taken by driving around Lough Gill, visiting Parke's Castle, and enjoying a meal at Markree Castle. Leave Sligo to the north and follow signposts for Enniskillen, Lough Derg, and Dromohair, which bring you to the northerly shore of **Lough Gill**. Glimpses of the lough through the trees give way to stunning lough views as the road hugs the shore and arrives at **Parke's Castle**, a fortified manor house whose ramparts and cottages (tearooms) have been restored. (Open Easter–Oct, tel: 071 64149.) In summer, you can take a boat trip on the lake which takes you around **Inishfree Island**. Leaving the castle, follow the lough into **Dromohair** where you pick up the Sligo road. After 5 kilometers, when the road divides, take a single-track lane to the right, which leads you down to the lakeside where John O'Connel's rowboat is tied to the pier. He lives by the lake and is sometimes available to row you to Inishfree Island. Returning to the main road, it's a short drive to **Collooney**, where you can partake of lunch or afternoon tea at **Markree Castle**.*

Leaving Sligo, travel north along the N15 to **Drumcliff Churchyard**, which has to be the most visited graveyard in Ireland. William Butler Yeats is buried here under the epitaph he composed, "Cast a cold eye on life, on death. Horseman, pass by!" In the background is the imposing **Benbulben Mountain**. Beyond the village, a left turn leads to **Lissadell,** home of the Gore-Booth sisters with whom Yeats was friendly. The 1830s Greek Revival-style house is full of curiosities and quite a sight to behold, but in need of an injection of capital to prevent its decay. While the sisters belonged to the landed gentry, Eva went on to become a poet and an important member of the suffragette movement. Constance was a commander in the 1916 uprising and the first elected female Labour Party M.P. Sir Henry Gore-Booth went off with his butler to explore the Antarctic in the 1880s. The bear that the butler shot is on the stairs. (*Open intermittently, usually Jun–Sep, closed Sun, tel: 071 63150.*)

Leaving Lissadell, continue north on the N15 for the 60-kilometer drive to Donegal, or follow a more circuitous route through Northern Ireland.

ALTERNATIVE ROUTE TO DONEGAL

*From Drumcliff churchyard, return towards Sligo and, at **Rathcormack**, turn left through the village of **Drum** to join the N16 as it travels east towards **Enniskillen**. Cross into Northern Ireland and take the first turn to your right following signposts to **Marble Arch Caves**. This extensive network of limestone chambers (billed as "over 300 million years of history") is most impressive. The tour includes an underground boat journey, walks through large illuminated chambers, galleries hung with remarkable stalactites, and a "Moses Walk" along a man-made passage through a lake where your feet are at the bottom of the pool and your head is at the same level as the water. Remember to dress warmly and take a sweater. It is best to telephone in advance because, if there has been a lot of rain, the caves are closed. (Open Mar–Oct, tel: 02866 348855.)*

*Leaving the hilltop cave complex, follow signposts for Enniskillen for 7 kilometers to **Florence Court**, an 18th-century mansion that was once the home of the Earls of Enniskillen. The opulent mansion is elegantly furnished and famous for the impressive rococo plasterwork on the ceilings. (Open Apr–Oct, tel: 01365 348249.) On leaving Florence Court, do **not** go into Enniskillen, but turn left onto the A46, following the scenic southern shore of **Lough Erne** for the 38-kilometer drive to Belleek.*

***Belleek**, on the far north shore of the lough, is famous for its ornate, creamy pottery: porcelain festooned with shamrocks or delicate, spaghetti-like strands woven into trellis-like plates. You can tour the visitors' center and then browse at the factory shop. (Open May–Sep.) Crossing back into the Republic, head for **Ballyshannon** and follow the wide N15 north for 23 kilometers to Donegal.*

Glencolumbkille

Donegal is a busy, bustling place, laid out around a diamond-shaped area surrounded by shops. Donegal is one of the best places to buy tweed goods—**Magees** sells a variety. The **Four Masters Bookshop** is a handy place to stock up on reading material. The ruins of **Donegal Castle** (open to the public), built in the 16th century by Hugh O'Donell, stand beside the Diamond.

Take the N56 west, hugging the coast, through **Dunkineely** and **Bruckless** to **Killybegs**, Ireland's major fishing port. Large trawlers from all over the world have replaced family fishing boats in the working harbor of this most enjoyable town. As you move west from Killybegs, the roads become more difficult, the landscape more rugged, the signposts less frequent, and—to complicate things—they are often written in Irish (Irish names are referenced in parentheses).

If the weather is fine, you can enjoy some spectacular scenery by following the brown signs that indicate a coastal route from **Kilcar** to **Carrick** (*An Charraig*), where you turn left (in the center of the village opposite the pub) for **Telin** (*Teilean*) and follow the brown signs for **Bunglar** and The Cliffs. As the narrow road winds up, down, and around the rocky, rolling landscape; you see several examples of traditional Irish cottages with small, thatched, pony-cart barns huddled next to them. The road narrows to a single track taking you along the very edge of the headlands to a viewpoint that overlooks the spot where the **Slieve League Cliffs** plummet into the sea. Walkers will love the magnificent walks along the headlands. This is not a trip to be taken in inclement weather.

Retrace your steps to Carrick and turn left towards **Glencolumbkille** (*Gleann Cholaim Cille*). The road enters the Owenwee Valley where you climb before descending into the glen. Drive through the scattered village to **Glencolumbkille Folk Village Museum** at the water's edge. Glencolumbkille is a place that gives one an appreciation of the survival of a people who endured hardship, famine, and debilitating emigration. By the 1960s, emigration was threatening to turn Glencolumbkille into a ghost town. In an effort to create some jobs, the parish priest, Father McDyer, formed a cooperative of the remaining local residents to develop a tourist industry by building a folk museum and holiday homes, and by encouraging local crafts. Tucked against a rocky hillside, the cottages that comprise the folk museum are grouped to form a traditional, tiny, village (*clachan*). Each cottage is a replica of those lived in by local people in each of three successive centuries. The thick, thatched roofs are tied down with heavy rope and anchored with stones, securing them from the harsh Atlantic winds. Inside, the little homes are furnished with period furniture and utensils. Locals guide you through the houses and give you snippets of local history. A handicraft shop sells Irish cottage crafts and the adjacent tearoom serves scones and piping hot tea. (*Open Easter–Oct, tours every half hour, tel: 073 30017.*)

Leaving Glencolumbkille, the narrow road climbs and dips through seemingly uninhabited, rugged countryside, where the views are often obscured by swirling mists as you climb the Glengesh Pass before dropping down into **Ardara**.

The North

The road skirts the coast and brings you to the twin fishing villages of **Portnoo** and **Nairn**, set amongst isolated beaches that truly have an "end-of-the-earth" quality about them. A short drive brings you to **Maas**, where you travel an extremely twisty road to the Gweebarra bridge taking you to **Lettermacaward** (*Leitir Mhic An Bhaird*) and on to **Dungloe** (*An Globhan Liath*). Nearby in **Burtonport** (*Ailt An Chorain*) more salmon and lobster are landed than at any other port. From here you drive north to **Kincasslagh**, and then it's on to **Annagary**, both tiny little communities that pride themselves on speaking the Irish language. A combination of wild, untamed scenery, villages that seem untouched by the 20th century, and narrow, curving roads in general disrepair, gives the feeling that the passage of time stopped many years ago in this isolated corner of Ireland.

Rejoin the N56 just south of **Gweedore** (*Gaoth Dobhair*) and follow it for a short distance as it swings inland paralleling a sea loch. As the main road swings to the right, continue straight up the mountain, following a narrow, winding road that brings you across peat bogs and purple, heather-covered moorlands inhabited only by sheep—to **Glenveagh National Park**, Ireland's largest, most natural, and most beautiful park. At its center lies a sheltered glen with a lake and mighty castle. The **Glenveagh Visitors' Centre** is well signposted and well disguised, being sunk into the ground with its roof camouflaged by peat and heather. There are displays, an audio-visual program, and a café (there's another at the castle), and it is here that you leave your car to take the minibus around the lake to **Glenveagh Castle** and its gardens. The heather and rose gardens, the rhododendrons, the laurels and pines, and busts and statues are all lovingly maintained, but the walled kitchen garden is especially memorable, with its profusion of flowers and tidy rows of vegetables divided by narrow, grass walkways. Surrounding this oasis of cultivated beauty are thousands of acres of wild countryside, where the largest herd of red deer in Ireland roam. Glenveagh Castle was built in 1870 by John Adair, using his American wife's money, in a fanciful gothic design that was popular in the later part of the century. The rooms have been beautifully restored and, for a small fee, you can tour the house (arrive by 2 pm if you're traveling in July and August). The Glenveagh estate was sold to the nation by the castle's second owner, Henry McIlhenny, who is largely responsible for the design of the gardens. (*Open Apr–Oct, tel: 074 37090.*)

Leaving the national park, turn right across the desolate boglands and heather-clad hills—your destination is **Glebe House and Gallery** (6 kilometers away) near the village of **Churchhill**. Derek Hill gave his home, Glebe House, and his art collection to the state, which remodeled the outbuildings to display his fine collection of paintings. Among the 300 paintings are works by Picasso, Bonnard, Yeats, Annigoni, and Pasmore. The decoration in the house includes William Morris papers and textiles, Victoriana, Donegal folk art, and Japanese and Islamic art. There is a tearoom in the courtyard. (*Open May–Sep, closed Fri, tel: 074 37071.*)

SIDE TRIP TO THE ROSGUILL PENINSULA AND TORY ISLAND

*If you would like to experience more Donegal coastal landscape, you can do no better than tour the **Rosguill Peninsula**, whose 25-kilometer Atlantic drive traces a wild, coastal route from **Rosapenna** through **Downies** and **Doagh** to **Tranarossan Bay** and back to Rosapenna. The road goes up and down, most of the time high above the ocean, then sweeps down to white, sandy beaches.*

*If you follow the coastal road west through **Gortahawk**, you come to **Meenlaragh** where you take the ferry to **Tory Island**, a windswept island where the inhabitants eke out a hard life farming and fishing. Sailing times of the ferryboat depend on the weather. If you want to visit the island, contact the Post Office in Meenlaragh. (Tel: 074 35165.)*

Giant's Causeway

From Glebe House, it is a 16-kilometer drive to **Letterkenny**. From the town, your route into Northern Ireland is well signposted to **Derry**. The N13 becomes the A2 as you cross the border and the pound sterling becomes the currency. Skirt Derry city on the **Foyle Bridge**, then follow the A2 to **Limavady** and the A37 for 21 kilometers to **Coleraine**.

Bushmills and the Giant's Causeway are well signposted from the outskirts of Coleraine. (One of the delights of traveling in Northern Ireland is that the roads are well paved and the signposting frequent and accurate.) **Bushmills** (see listings) is famous for its whiskey—a whiskey spelled with an "e"—of which Special Old Black Bush is the best. A tour of the factory demonstrates how they turn barley and water into whiskey and rewards you with a sample of the classic drink to fortify you for your visit to the nearby Giant's Causeway. (*Open daily, tel: 028 2073 1521.*)

In the last century, the **Giant's Causeway** was thought to be one of the wonders of the world. Formed from basaltic rock, which cooled and split into regular, prismatic shapes, it stepped out to sea to build an irregular honeycomb of columns some 70,000,000 years ago. More romantic than scientific fact is the legend that claims the causeway was built by the Irish giant, Finn MacCool, to get at his rival in Scotland. Do not expect the columns to be tall, for they are not—it is their patterns that make them interesting, not their size.

The first stop on a visit to the causeway is the **Giant's Causeway Centre**, where the facts and legends about the causeway are well presented in an audio-visual theater. (*Open all year, tel: 028 2073 1159, email: unavsm@smtp.ntrust.org.uk.*) A minibus takes you to the head of the causeway, where you follow the path past formations called "Honeycomb," "Wishing Well," "Giant's Granny," "King and his Nobles," "Port na Spaniagh" (where gold and silver treasure from the Spanish Armada ship, *Girona*, was found in 1967), and "Lovers' Leap" and then up the wooden staircase to the headlands, where you walk back to the visitors' center along the clifftops. (It's a 5-kilometer walk and you can truly say you have seen the causeway, if you complete the circuit.)

Leaving the causeway, turn right along the coast to visit the ruins of the nearby **Dunluce Castle**, a romantic ruin clinging to a wave-lashed cliff with a great cave right underneath. This was the main fort of the Irish MacDonnells, chiefs of Antrim. It fell into ruin after the kitchen (and cooks!) fell into the sea during a storm. (*Open Apr–Sep.*)

Retrace your route down the B146 and, at the causeway gates, turn left along the coast road. Watch carefully for a small plaque at the side of the road pointing out the very meager ruins of **Dunseverick Castle**. Dunseverick was at the northernmost end of the Celtic road where the Celts crossed to and from Scotland.

Shortly after joining the A2, turn left for **Port Braddon**. The road winds down to the sea where a hamlet of gaily painted houses and a church nestles around a sheltered harbor. As you stand in front of the smallest church in Ireland, the long, sandy beaches of **Whitepark Bay** stretch before you.

Carrick-a-Rede Rope Bridge

Farther along the coast, a narrow road winds down to the very picturesque **Ballintoy Harbour**, a sheltered haven for boats surrounded by small, jagged, rocky islands. At the first road bend after leaving Ballintoy village, turn sharp left for the **Carrick-a-Rede Rope Bridge**. This is one of the famous things to do in Ireland: walk high above the sea across a narrow, swinging bridge of planks and ropes that joins a precipitous cliff to a rocky island. Hardy fishermen, whose cottages and nets nestle in a sheltered cleft on the island and whose fragile wooden boats bob in the ocean below, still use the bridge. (*Open mid-Apr–mid-Sep.*)

Life in the nearby holiday town of **Ballycastle** centers around the beach, fishing, and golf. Cross the river and turn onto the A2 to **Ballyvoy**. If the weather is clear, turn left for the scenic drive to Cushendun around **Torr Head**. The narrow road, barely wide enough for two cars to pass, switches back across the headlands and corkscrews down the cliffside, offering spectacular views of the rugged coastline and the distant Mull of Kintyre in Scotland.

Nestled by the seashore, the pretty village of **Cushendun** has a National Trust Shop, an excellent place to buy high-quality souvenirs. When you leave Cushendun, the landscape softens and the road, thankfully, returns to a more manageable width. You are now entering the **Glens of Antrim**, where lush, green fields and a succession of beautiful views present themselves. At **Cushendall** you can detour into **Glenariff Forest Park**, the queen of the glens with a series of waterfalls plunging down a gorge traversed by a scenic path crossing rustic bridges. Thackeray described this glen as "Switzerland in miniature." (*Open all year.*)

After your return to the coast road, **Carnlough**, a pretty seaside and fishing town, soon comes into view, its little white harbor full of bobbing boats. The **Londonderry Arms** was once a coaching inn and now is a hotel and restaurant.

Nearby **Glenarm** is the oldest of the coastal villages, dating back to the time of King John. The pseudo-gothic castle is the home of the Earl of Antrim, part of whose demesne, **Glenarm Forest**, climbs up from the glen and is open to the public. (*Open all year.*)

Limestone cliffs present themselves as you approach **Larne**, a sizable seaport whose Viking origins are lost amongst more modern commercial developments. Wend your way through this busy port town, following the A2 to **Whitehead**. Nearby **Carrickfergus** is the oldest town in Northern Ireland. **Carrickfergus Castle**, a sturdy Norman castle overlooking the boat-filled harbor, was built as a stronghold in 1178 by John de Courcy after his invasion of Ulster; then taken by King John after a siege in 1210; fell to the Scots in 1316; and was captured by the French in 1760. Life-sized models and a film recreate the castle's turbulent past. (*Open all year.*)

Leaving Carrickfergus, a 12-kilometer drive along the A2 and M2/M1 whisks you through, or into, **Belfast** (see listings), where the A1 will take you south through **Newry** and into the Republic. Or, if you are staying near the Antrim coast for several days of leisurely sightseeing, take the M2 to the A26, which quickly returns you to that area.

Carrickfergus Castle

The North

Places to Stay

The Dunraven Arms stands on the broad main street of this attractive town. With its uniformed staff, check-in desk, and lovely bedrooms it is has more the feel of a country house than a hotel. Smartly decorated throughout, its attractive antique furniture adds to the old-world feeling. The large, informal bar is a gathering place for locals and residents alike, but if you want a few quiet moments, there are several private lounges with comfortable chairs overlooking the garden. While the bedrooms in the old hostelry have lots of character we prefer the utter peace and quiet of the new wing that stretches down long corridors behind the inn into the garden. We love their spaciousness, large bathrooms and garden views. There's a good few of them that have antique four poster beds and fireplaces as well. The brasserie style dining room serves well priced food. There's always a traditional roast on the trolley to be carved at your table. For more casual dining visit the hotel's cozy restaurant, The Inn Between, in a quaint thatched cottage across the street. Enjoy the health center with its swimming pool, gymnasium and array of spa treatment rooms. The hotel specializes in making golfing, equestrian, and fishing arrangements for guests. *Directions:* Adare is on the N21, 40 km from Shannon airport, which makes it an ideal first or last stop in Ireland if you are traveling in the southwest.

DUNRAVEN ARMS
Owners: Louis & Bryan Murphy
Adare, Co Limerick, Ireland
Tel: (061) 396633, Fax: (061) 396541
86 Rooms, Double: €200–€335*
*Breakfast not included: €20, Service: 12.5%
Dinner: €46
Open: all year, Credit cards: all major
www.karenbrown.com/dunravenarms.html

Just down a country lane from the charming little ferry that plies its way to Waterford across the Barrow estuary, Dunbrody House was the onetime home of the Marquis of Donegal. Catherine and Kevin Dundon have transformed it from a private house to stylish top-class hotel complete with spa and cookery school. Kevin and his team produce food that is as exquisite to look at as it is gorgeous to eat. The house is a delightful blend of contemporary and country house—lots of scrumptious public rooms and some particularly spacious bedrooms, such as 300 with it's French windows opening up to the garden. Top of the line bathrooms are the order of the day and the house is wheelchair friendly. A resident corgi and labrador are on hand to escort you on invigorating walks that encompass terrific views of the Barrow Estuary. Be sure to visit the hens and stroll around the large organic fruit and vegetable gardens. Explore the wild and beautiful Hook Peninsula, visiting Europe's oldest lighthouse, and take the ferry to Waterford and its famous crystal factory. *Directions:* From Wexford take the R733 to Arthurstown. Dunbrody House is on your left as you approach the village. If arriving from Waterford, take the Passage East Ferry to Ballyhack. Turn right off the ferry and go 2 km (through Arthurstown) to Dunbrody House, which is on your right as you go up the hill.

DUNBRODY HOUSE
Owners: Catherine & Kevin Dundon
Arthurstown, Co Wexford, Ireland
Tel: (051) 389600, Fax: (051) 389601
20 Rooms, Double: €245–€425
Dinner: €60
Open: all year, Credit cards: all major
Ireland Blue Book
www.karenbrown.com/dunbrody.html

The Wicklow Mountains offer some of the finest walks in Ireland and there is no finer place to stay in the area than Ballyknocken House. Hospitality is Catherine Fulvio's keynote, with good baking and cooking providing the backbone for fine evening meals and decadent breakfasts. The house has been completely renovated and returned it to its original 1850s style so that it has all the charm of days gone by along with 21st-century plumbing. Five bedrooms have Victorian tubs with showers. All rooms are named after local places, the pronunciation of which may prove challenging! My favorites are Knocknaphrumpha and Aghowle at the front of the house with views over the garden. Catherine has a cooking school in the adjacent renovated milking sheds and guests often book one of her hour long classes on the baking of brown bread, scones and soda bread. If you want to stay for several days consider renting the two bedroom apartment over the cookery school. The Wicklow Way, Ireland's famous hill-walking route, is close by. If you are not up to long walks, the dogs will accompany you through the hills behind the farm—but be sure to have directions with you as they have a habit of depositing you at a neighbor's farm! *Directions:* Take the N11 south from Dublin towards Wicklow for 42 km to Ashford (just before Rathnew). Turn right immediately after the Petrol station up a steep hill and follow this road for almost 5 km to Ballyknocken House on your right.

BALLYKNOCKEN HOUSE
Owners: Catherine & Claudio Fulvio
Ashford, Glenealy, Co Wicklow, Ireland
Tel: (0404) 44627, Fax: (0404) 44696
7 Rooms, Double: €120–€130
1 Apartment: €600–€750 weekly
Dinner: €39 (not Sun or Mon)
Open: Feb to Nov, Credit cards: MC, VS
www.karenbrown.com/ballyknocken.html

Clone House was originally built in the 1650s and rebuilt around 1805 after burning down in the 1798 Rebellion. Now it's the home of Carla and Jeff Watson and their 3 children, with plenty of room for both family and guests. Make yourself at home in the drawing room, try your hand at the piano in the cozy music room, browse Carla's cookbooks in the parlor, or work out in the well-equipped gym. Carla uses fresh local produce cooked in Italian Tuscan style with lots of tomatoes, wine, porcini mushrooms and extra virgin olive oil. Fresh baked foccacia bread is always served with dinner. For breakfast, as well as the traditional Irish fry and soda breads, there are scones and a variety of sweet breads. Vale of Avoca is the largest bedroom with a skylight above the bed, a peat-burning fireplace, shower in the bathroom, and beautiful views of the garden. I also liked the coziness of Clara Vale with its rustic brick wall, red velvet drapes, bed hangings, fireplace, and view of the garden. Folks who admire what Jeff has done with his 5 acres of garden often head for Powerscourt Gardens. Nearby Avoca village is the Ballykissangel of the television series. The monastic settlement of Glendalough is interesting to visit, as are the beaches along Brittas Bay. *Directions:* In Aughrim, take the R4747 towards Tinahely. While in the village turn left at the low black and yellow-striped wall, then follow signs to the house. The entrance is on the right.

CLONE HOUSE
Owners: Carla & Jeff Watson
Aughrim, Co Wicklow, Ireland
Tel: (0402) 36121, Fax: (0402) 36029
7 Rooms, Double: €160–€200
Dinner: €55 to €66
Open: all year, Credit cards: MC, VS
Hidden Ireland
www.karenbrown.com/clone.html

Bagenalstown is sometimes signposted Muine Bheag, which can lead to a certain amount of confusion in reaching Kilgraney House. But the effort put into finding it is worthwhile, for this is not your run-of-the-mill Irish country house—it's more like "Architectural Digest" than "Country Life." With its crisp lines and whimsical touches, the decor is the brainchild of your hosts, designers Bryan Leech and Martin Marley. After working abroad, Bryan and Martin returned to Ireland. Kilgraney House was put together with a touch of whimsy and artistic flair, traditional Irish antiques being added to their overseas treasures. The same attention to detail was lavished on the spotless modern bathrooms. The cooking is modern and imaginative and incorporates seasonal fruits, vegetables and herbs from the enclosed kitchen garden. In another courtyard there's a medicinal herb garden with nine raised beds in Irish oak timber, each planted with herbs suitable for treating a specific part of the body. In a converted apple house, there's an aromatherapy centre offering an all-encompassing selection of massages, facials and herbal wraps. *Directions:* Take the N9 from Dublin to Royal Oak (south of Carlow), turn left into Bagenalstown (Muine Bheag), and right in the village for the 6-km drive to Kilgraney crossroads. Turn right (signposted) and Kilgraney House is the first entrance on the left (a 2-hour drive).

KILGRANEY HOUSE
Owners: Bryan Leech & Martin Marley
Bagenalstown, Co Carlow, Ireland
Tel: (059) 9775283, Fax: (059) 9775595
4 Rooms, Double: €110–€190
2 Apartments: €350–€400 weekly
Dinner: €45 (not Mon to Thu: Mar to Jun & Sep to Oct)
Closed: Dec & Jan, Credit cards: all major
www.karenbrown.com/kilgraneyhouse.html

A stay at Echo Lodge is all about eating fabulous food in the Mustard Seed Restaurant. Head chef Toni Schwartz's four-course table d'hote menu leaves you spoilt for choice. Owner Dan Mullane is usually on hand to explain your choices in delicious detail. Much of the produce is home grown—the organic fruit and vegetable gardens are in terraces behind the hotel. The atmosphere is convivial, Dan and his staff really go the extra mile to make you welcome. Outside diners give a real buzz to the place in an evening. Bedrooms range from quirky country house to elegant suites. There's a specially designed wheelchair-friendly room. A cute little sauna and a small exercise room are also available. The quiet village location is well suited for touring the southwest and playing the several surrounding golf courses. The delightful town of Adare is a 15-minute drive away and the surrounding peaceful countryside offers lots of opportunities for horse riding, fishing, clay pigeon shooting, and antique hunting. *Directions:* From Adare take the N21, Killarney road for 2 km and turn left for Ballingarry. In the village take the Newcastle West road for 500 meters and Echo Lodge is on your right.

THE MUSTARD SEED AT ECHO LODGE
Owner: Dan Mullane
Ballingarry, Co Limerick, Ireland
Tel: (069) 68508, Fax: (069) 68511
14 Rooms, Double: €190–€310
Dinner: €55
Closed: first two weeks of Feb, Credit cards: all major
Ireland Blue Book
www.karenbrown.com/echolodge.html

Whitepark House has a perfect location on the prettiest part of the north Antrim coast between the famed Giant's Causeway and the precarious Carrick-a-Rede rope bridge. A narrow pathway leads down to the cluster of white cottages and tiny church that make up the much-photographed village of Portbraddan—on a sunny day one could easily imagine oneself in Greece. On a clear day you can see the Rathlin Island lighthouse and the distant Scottish islands of Islay and Jura. Small wonder that Siobhan and Bob love the area and are keen for guests to really enjoy it and their home, Whitepark House, which was built in 1735 and extended in the early 1900s. Bob and Siobhan are inveterate travelers—India, Japan, Sri Lanka, Thailand, Africa. Fascinating mementos of their travels are artfully displayed alongside masses of leafy green houseplants, which flourish under Bob's tender care. Eat breakfast in the bay window in the open-plan hallway and toast your toes by the fire in the spacious sitting room. Upstairs, three spacious bedrooms share a bathroom and additional downstairs toilet—robes are provided. Bob is happy to drive walkers to the Giant's Causeway and welcomes them home after a 13-kilometer coastal walk with homemade biscuits and tea. *Directions:* Whitepark House is on the coast road 6.5 km east of the Giant's Causeway and just over 1.5 km west of Ballintoy.

WHITEPARK HOUSE
Owners: Siobhan & Bob Isles
Ballintoy
Co Antrim BT45 6NH, Northern Ireland
Tel: (028) 2073 1482, Fax: none
3 Rooms, Double: £70
Open: all year, Credit cards: MC, VS
www.karenbrown.com/whitepark.html

Stella Maris has a fabulous location on the shores of Bunatrahir Bay where white topped waves cascade across the rocks and windswept sandy beaches stretch towards the rugged cliffs of Downpatrick Head. Built in 1853 as coastguard headquarters it later served as a convent and then as a school. Most recently new life, as a boutique hotel, has been breathed into these sturdy buildings by Frances Kelly and Terence McSweeney. It's a stylish place with a pleasing blend of traditional and modern décor. Quite the best place to enjoy the ever-changing seascape is from the conservatory built all along the front of the building to maximize the panoramic ocean views. Dinner is cooked by Frances and enjoyed in the dining room made up of four intimate little cottage rooms—then it's back to the conservatory for coffee and drinks. Almost all of the bedrooms are ocean facing and come in queens and kings/twins all named after local and famous golf courses. The many miles of wild County Mayo coastline are yours to explore. Be sure to visit nearby Ceide Fields, an excavated Stone-Age settlement with walls older than the pyramids. *Directions:* Stella Maris is located on the ocean, 25 km west of Ballina and 2 km west of Ballycastle.

STELLA MARIS COUNTRY HOUSE HOTEL
Owners: Frances Kelly & Terry McSweeney
Ballycastle, Co Mayo, Ireland
Tel: 011-353-96-43322, Fax: 011-353-96-43965
11 Rooms, Double: €190–€240
Dinner: €45
Open: Easter to mid-Oct, Credit cards: MC, VS
Ireland Blue Book
www.karenbrown.com/stellamarisire.html

We visited Gorman's at the insistence of Peter Haden, of Gregans Castle. We completely agree with everything he stated in his email to us: "…(This property) has a spectacular location out on the remotest part of the Dingle Peninsula overlooking Smerwick Harbour and out to the Atlantic—wild, savage scenery surrounds. The building is quite new and certainly not quaint, but the moment you step inside, there is a wonderful feeling of warmth generated by the most genuine greeting, open fires, sunny color schemes, and very comfortable furnishings. The tea and homemade biscuits make you immediately relax and feel at home. There are nine large, well-furnished bedrooms, all with fabulous views and good bathrooms with buckets of hot water and all the little extras. The dining room is designed to take advantage of the views, and we had dinner watching the sun set on the Atlantic horizon. Food is fine without being famous, and service is very friendly. Rarely before have I stayed in a place where I had such a good feeling of genuine friendliness and warmth from the owners, who are dedicated to providing the best for everyone. What more can I say?" Not a thing! *Directions:* Go through Dingle town keeping the harbor on your left. At the roundabout west of town, go straight (signpost An Fheothanach)—Gorman's is 13 km on. After about 8 km the road forks: stay left and you come back to the coast—the sea is on your right and Gorman's is on your left.

GORMAN'S CLIFFTOP HOUSE
Owners: Sile & Vincent Gorman
Glaise Bheag
Ballydavid, (Baile na nGall) Dingle Peninsula
Co Kerry, Ireland
Tel & Fax: (066) 9155 162
9 Rooms, Double: €150–€190
Dinner: €38-€50 (not Sun)
Closed: Christmas, Credit cards: MC, VS
www.karenbrown.com/gormans.html

This tall, bright-white Victorian house set amidst lush gardens rimming the shores of Bantry Bay is a most hospitable hotel. Run by long-time owner Kathleen O'Sullivan the atmosphere is friendly and informal, which accounts, I am sure, for the large number of guests who return here year after year. The sitting room/bar, pretty in soft pinks and blues with light-wood furniture, offers plenty of places to sit in snug little corners. For those in search of peace and quiet there is an old-fashioned parlor/TV room. The dining room is cleverly divided into several areas which creates a most enjoyable experience. Be sure to request a room at the front of the house for several have tiny glimpses of the ocean through the trees at the bottom of the garden. We especially enjoyed the décor, location and spaciousness of rooms in the new wing. Two garden view rooms on the ground floor have been especially equipped for the handicapped. The scenery hereabouts is spectacular. If you have time, wander off the main roads to explore the Beara Peninsula with its views of barren, rocky mountains tumbling into the sea. A "must visit" is nearby Garinish Island, a spectacular garden with trees, shrubs, and plants from every part of the world. Just down the road is Bantry House, a grand mansion that is well worth a visit. *Directions:* Seaview House Hotel is located in Ballylickey on the N71 between Bantry and Glengarriff.

SEAVIEW HOUSE HOTEL
Owner: Kathleen O'Sullivan
Ballylickey, Co Cork, Ireland
Tel: (027) 50462/50073, Fax: (027) 51555
26 Rooms, Double: €140–€180
Dinner: €45
Open: mid-Mar to mid-Nov, Credit cards: all major
www.karenbrown.com/seaviewhouse.html

Olive and Paddy O'Gorman have a relaxed, easygoing attitude to life. They welcome guests to the wing of their commodious farmhouse nestled in the pretty Nire Valley, an area of Ireland off the beaten tourist path and noted for its beautiful scenery. Knowing that you deserve the best, request one of Olive's premier rooms with Jacuzzi tub and shower. Olive takes great pride in her bedrooms not only matching the bedspread and drapes with the wallpaper but taking it so far to see that each room has cups and saucers that match the room's colorful decor. Olive finds it no problem at all to juggle her family and a houseful of guests, chatting with them over tea and cake when they arrive, feeding them copious breakfasts, packing tempting lunches, arranging for them to go walking and feeding them dinner in the conservatory on their return. Guests come to this quiet corner of County Waterford to walk the Comeragh Mountains and experience Irish farmhouse hospitality. If the outdoor pursuits of fishing, pony-trekking, and walking are not your cup of tea, you can drive to Lismore, Cashel, or over The Vee, returning in time for a visit to one of the nearby pubs for a late-night Irish music session. *Directions:* From Clonmel or Dungarven follow the R671 to Ballymacarbry. Four Mile Water is signposted to your right just before you reach Ballymacarbry if you are coming from Clonmel or just after to your left if you are coming from Dungarven.

GLASHA
Owners: Olive & Paddy O'Gorman
Ballymacarbry, Via Clonmel
Co Waterford, Ireland
Tel & Fax: (052) 36108
8 Rooms, Double: €100–€120
Dinner: €25-€35 (not Sun)
Closed: Christmas, Credit cards: none
www.karenbrown.com/glasha.html

People just love Temple House and no wonder. Roderick and Helena Perceval just know how to treat guests and make them feel at ease and completely at home. And what a home it is—my house would fit in the entrance hall where Roderick keeps the "wellies", fishing paraphernalia, and inclement weather gear. And that's just the tip of the iceberg for beyond lie rooms of enormous proportions. One bedroom is aptly named the half acre. Another is the twins' room because it has two of everything—all pleasingly idiosyncratic and just bursting with character. Furniture made for the house is still here along with some of the original carpets and draperies. Just to complete the picture it always seems that I have the most interesting dinner conversations with my fellow guests around the polished dining room table and, of course, the food is always excellent. As for what to do during the day—some folks never leave the estate: there's a vast lake for fishing, a lakeside castle built by the Knights Templar in 1200, a huge walled garden, and miles of walking. The Percevals have lived here since 1665 and there are some wonderful stories of ancestors' exploits. *Directions:* From Sligo take the N4 to the N17 (Galway road). The house is signpost to the left 0.5km south of Ballinacarrow.

TEMPLE HOUSE
Owners: Roderick & Helena Perceval
Ballinacarrow, Ballymote
Co Sligo, Ireland
Tel: (071) 9183329, Fax: (071) 9183808
6 Rooms, Double: €160–€190
1 Cottage: €900 weekly
Dinner: €42 (not Sun)
Open: Apr to Nov, Credit cards: MC, VS
Hidden Ireland
www.karenbrown.com/templehouse.html

Ballinkeele House was built for the Maher family in 1840, and Margaret and John are the fourth generation of Mahers to call this heritage house home. Set amidst 350 acres of parklike grounds, the house has all the solid quality of a grand home built in the early Victorian period: big rooms, fine ceilings, decorative doors, quality in every detail. Apart from the addition of heating and modern bathrooms, the house has not changed over the years. Soft Oriental rugs dress the flagstone entry, which is warmed by a huge, old-fashioned stove, and grand oil paintings and family portraits adorn the walls. Antique furniture graces the cozy drawing room and enormous dining room where guests enjoy delicious candlelit dinners. The Master Bedroom is a particularly large room decorated in soft red and beiges with an impressive four-poster bed sitting center stage. For recreation there are walks through the estate and croquet on the lawn. Settle in for several nights and enjoy County Wexford—historic Wexford's Georgian theater, home to the October Opera Festival; the Wexford Wildlife Reserve, famous for its wintering wildfowl; and the National Heritage Park with its old Irish buildings. The Mahers have bicycles for guests. The port of Rosslare is a 40-minute drive away. *Directions:* From Dublin take the N11, Wexford road, to Gorey. Turn left at the traffic lights for Wexford (R741) for 30 km and the 5-km drive to Ballinkeele House is signposted on your right.

BALLINKEELE HOUSE
Owners: Margaret & John Maher
Ballymurn, Enniscorthy
Co Wexford, Ireland
Tel: (053) 9138105, Fax: (053) 9138468
5 Rooms, Double: €150–€180
Dinner: €46 (not Tues)
Open: Feb to Nov, Credit cards: all major
Hidden Ireland
www.karenbrown.com/ballinkeelehouse.html

Ballynahinch Castle, former home of the O'Flaherty chieftains, a pirate queen and a maharajah, has enjoyed a long and chequered history. The heart of this friendly hotel is the bar with its old brick floor and little tables surrounded by Windsor chairs. Here a long table displays the "catch of the day" and fisherfolk hang the keys that give them access to the little huts on their fishing beats—no standing out in the rain when fishing here. The beats are so close to the house that folks return to the bar for lunch (packed lunches are also available). Bar food is served in the evening for those who are not inclined to partake of a more formal meal in the dining room whose windows overlook the river. Bedrooms come in three varieties: standard, superior, and luxury, which at Ballynahinch Castle means large, larger, and largest. I particularly enjoyed my standard room, Oranmore, and preferred its low-ceiling coziness to the more spacious superior rooms with their higher ceilings. However, I was very taken with the new, luxurious riverside rooms with their grand beds, walk-through dressing rooms, separate baths and showers, and fireplaces. The natural beauty of Connemara is on your doorstep. Often guests never leave the hotel's property, spending their days wandering through the 450 acres of grounds or by the fire with a book. *Directions:* From Galway take the N59 Clifden for 68 km and turn left for Roundstone. The hotel is on your right after 4 km.

BALLYNAHINCH CASTLE
Manager: Patrick O'Flaherty
Ballynahinch, Connemara
Co Galway, Ireland
Tel: (095) 31006, Fax: (095) 31085
40 Rooms, Double: €200–€400*
Service: 10%
Dinner: €50
Closed: Feb, Credit cards: all major
www.karenbrown.com/ballynahinch.html

With the bare limestone crags of The Burren sheltering its back and a panoramic view of Ballyvaughan Bay to the towering cliffs of Black Head in front, Drumcreehy House commands an enviable rural position just outside the picturesque village of Ballyvaughan. Bernadette and Armin designed this house to look as old as possible while including all modern amenities. To add to the traditional feel, they have furnished the sitting room and dining room with antiques, and all the bedrooms with old pine. Spring Gentian and Dog Violet are especially spacious with larger shower rooms, and along with Cowslip and Primrose enjoy spectacular views across the bay to Black Head. If you are not up to stairs request a room in the adjacent two bedroom cottage—perfect for families. Enjoy a cooked breakfast in the sunny yellow breakfast room where a table is laden with fruit, cereal, cheeses, and meats. Bernadette and Armin will advise you on where to go for dinner. Shannon is an hour's drive away, making this an ideal first or last night on your trip, but stay longer and explore The Burren and the Cliffs of Moher. *Directions:* From Shannon take the N18 to Ennis, the N85 towards Ennistymon, and the first right (R476) through Corofin and on towards Kilfenora. At the ruined castle turn right onto the R480 for Ballyvaughan and go about 7 miles to the village. At Hylands Hotel, turn right for Galway. Drive out for 1 mile and it's the yellow house on the right.

DRUMCREEHY HOUSE
Owners: Bernadette & Armin Grefkes
Ballyvaughan, Co Clare, Ireland
Tel: (065) 7077377, Fax: (065) 7077379
10 Rooms, Double: €80–€100
Open: all year, Credit cards: MC, VS
www.karenbrown.com/drumcreehy.html

Gregans Castle is only 57 kilometers from Shannon airport, so if you are heading north or west, this is the perfect spot to begin your stay in Ireland. This is not an imposing castle, but a sprawling manor house set in lovely gardens in a lush green valley completely surrounded by The Burren, with its "moonscapes" of gray limestone and scattered alpine and arctic plants. While there are several comfortable lounges to congregate in, my preference is the beamed Corkscrew bar with its blazing turf fire. Lunch is served here, and in the evening guests gather for a drink and a chat. From the dining room, where tables are reserved for all guests for dinner each night, windows frame outstanding views of The Burren sweeping down to the edge of Galway Bay. On a recent visit I really liked Gleninagh—a standard twin room with a particularly nice bathroom, Mina's room—a superior queen-bedded room in the oldest part of the house facing Galway Bay, and the three garden suites with their private patios and brand new bathrooms. Local attractions include the Ailwee Caves, full of stalactites and stalagmites, and the Cliffs of Moher. *Directions:* From Shannon take the N18 to Ennis, the N85 towards Ennistymon, the first right (R476) through Corofin, and on towards Kilfenora. At the ruined castle turn right onto the R480 towards Ballyvaughan and, as you crest The Burren, you see the hotel in the valley below.

GREGANS CASTLE
Owners: Frederieke & Simon Haden
Ballyvaughan, Co Clare, Ireland
Tel: (065) 7077 005, Fax: (065) 7077 111
21 Rooms, Double: €210–€290
Dinner: from €36
Open: Mar 31 to Oct 28, Credit cards: all major
Ireland Blue Book
www.karenbrown.com/gregans.html

Rosemary and Brian McAuley had Dunauley designed to take advantage of the spectacular view of the island-dotted Bantry Bay, aptly framed by a wall of windows in the living/dining room. Three double-bedded bedrooms, each with en suite shower room, are found on the same level as the living room. Downstairs is an additional bedroom with a magnificent view. A snug one bedroom apartment (queen plus single beds) has its own entrance and can be rented on a weekly basis. Guests enjoy both the living room and its particularly fine view as they sit round the fire in the evening and while tucking into an ample breakfast before setting out on a day's sightseeing. Breakfast is the only meal Rosemary serves, and guests usually drive into town for dinner. The drive from Bantry to Glengarriff gives a taste of the rugged landscape and exotic flora that you find in this part of Ireland. From the town you can take a boat to Garinish Island, a lush collection of interesting shrubs, trees, and flowers from all over the world. For over three years a hundred men worked to make Arran Bryce's garden, caseta, and temple; but financial hardships precluded the building of his home. *Directions:* From the center of Bantry follow white signs for the hospital through the one-way system and up the hill. Pass a church on the right and continue on this road till you see Dunauley signposted to the right—keep going uphill to the house.

DUNAULEY
Owners: Rosemary & Brian McAuley
Seskin
Bantry, Co Cork, Ireland
Tel & Fax: (027) 50290
4 Rooms, Double: €80–€90
1 apartment (€350–€450 weekly)
Open: May to Sep, Credit cards: none
www.karenbrown.com/dunauley.html

Ash-Rowan is the relaxed, very friendly, unpretentious home of Sam and Evelyn Hazlett—an excellent choice for a bed and breakfast while staying in the northern capital. A varied choice of breakfasts sets you up for the day—opt for organic porridge flavored with Drambuie and cream served with pancakes; Irish scramble with eggs, chopped bacon, and mushrooms, or the Ulster Fry, the ultimate cooked breakfast which the menu warns is not for the faint hearted. Vegetarians should try the flambéed mushrooms or vegetarian omlette. It's a climb to the top of the house (no large cases!) but worth it to secure one of the choice rooms (7 and 8) that offer more spacious quarters. All the rooms have TVs, phones, bathrobes, and hospitality trays with biscuits, teas, coffee, and instant soups. Beds are made with crisply starched linen sheets and pillowcases. The location, near the university, is perfect for strolling into the city and taxis are inexpensive for a night out on the town. Peruse the papers and the tourist literature in the wonderfully cluttered conservatory then seek out Sam or Evelyn to set you up with sightseeing venues for the day. *Directions:* From central Belfast take Dublin Road to Shaftesbury Square. Go through Bradbury Place onto University Road. Pass Queen's University on the left and go straight through the traffic lights into Malone Road. Windsor Avenue is the fifth avenue on your right.

ASH-ROWAN
Owners: Evelyn & Sam Hazlett
12 Windsor Avenue
Belfast BT9 6EE Northern Ireland
Tel: (028) 9066 1758, Fax: (028) 9066 3227
5 Rooms, Double: £89–£98
Closed: Christmas & New Year, Credit cards: MC, VS
www.karenbrown.com/ashrowan.html

John and Ann are particularly gregarious hosts, perhaps influenced by their close proximity to the Blarney stone, said to confer the "gift of the gab." John would have you believe that you can tour the entire south of Ireland from their guesthouse. While this is somewhat of an exaggeration, it certainly is an ideal base for visiting Cork, Cobh, Kinsale, as well as enjoying a day in Blarney where the castle's lovely grounds and Blarney woolen mills are great attractions. While Ashlee Lodge may seem unremarkable from the road, the place is full of surprises. Comfortable bedrooms can all be either twin or king, with large TVs and CD players. They come in three sizes: executive—good size rooms with shower over the tub, garden—larger rooms with Jacuzzi bathtubs, or master—very large rooms with sitting area and Jacuzzi bathtubs. One bedroom is totally wheelchair friendly. There's also an upstairs deck with a hot tub. Drinks are served from the honesty bar in the evening and the light and airy breakfast room (lots of choices as well as a cooked Irish breakfast) doubles as the restaurant in the evening. Golf is endemic hereabouts and John will gladly arrange tee times and transportation. If you want to travel without a car, airport pickup can be arranged. Handily the bus to Blarney and Cork runs by the front door. *Directions:* Ashlee Lodge is located in Tower, 2 km west of Blarney. The house is on the R617—the Blarney to Killarney Road.

✳ ☕ 🖕 CREDIT ⛰ ☎ 🐕 P ⑂ 🚭 ✿ 🖼 ♿ ✝ 🏃 ⚓

ASHLEE LODGE
Owner: John and Anne O'Leary
Blarney, Co Cork, Ireland
Tel: (021) 4385346, Fax: (021) 4385726
10 Rooms, Double: €140–€220
Dinner: €35 (not Sun or Mon)
Closed: Christmas & New Year
Credit cards: MC, VS
www.karenbrown.com/ashlee.html

Bobbie Smith's home reflects her welcoming, easygoing personality. Filled with mellow old furniture, books, pictures, and family mementos, the Old Rectory is very much a lived-in, comfortable family home for Bobbie and her three daughters. Guests are welcomed with a reviving pot of tea in the homey drawing room, and it is here that they chat with fellow guests before dinner, which is taken by candlelight round the long, gleaming dining room table. Bedrooms have the same traditional family feel and range from a snug twin to two spacious rooms, one with a carved four-poster and the other with a splendid Victorian bed with turned posts decorating the foot and headboard. All have en suite shower rooms and there's an extra "bath" so that those who love to soak can do so in a claw-foot tub. The area is perfect for cycling; and holidays that include cycle hire, airport pickup, and baggage transportation can be arranged. Those who prefer to stick to their car will find Kilkenny with its castle, fine old shops, and lovely buildings just a 20-minute drive away. Day trips can be taken to Wexford, Kildare, and Glendalough. *Directions:* Take the N9 from Dublin to Royal Oak (south of Carlow), turn left into Bagenalstown, and right in the village for the 6-km drive to Lorum Old Rectory.

LORUM OLD RECTORY
Owner: Bobbie Smith
Kilgreaney, Bagenalstown
Borris
Co Carlow, Ireland
Tel: (059) 9775282, Fax: (059) 9775455
5 Rooms, Double: €150–€160
Dinner: €45
Closed: Nov to Feb, Credit cards: MC, VS
Hidden Ireland
www.karenbrown.com/lorumoldrectory.html

Bruckless House was built in the mid-18th century and lived in by the Cassidy brothers, traders and merchants who sold guns to Napoleon and pickled herrings to Wellington in Portugal. Later the house was owned by a passionate Communist, Commander Fforde, who is remembered for his many good works in the area. Continuing the tradition of colorful owners, Clive and Joan Evans moved here after spending many years in Hong Kong. This lovely home has the most marvelous location, set in wooded acres with garden paths leading down to the rocky shoreline of Bruckless Bay. Colorful Oriental rugs warm the flagstone entryway and mementos of the Evans' years abroad blend with comfortable family antiques. A log fire warms the dining room on chilly mornings as guests breakfast together round the long polished table. Bedrooms are found in what was once the children's wing up the back staircase. Nanny's Room is a delightful twin-bedded room with an en suite bathroom with a power shower over the tub, and a double-bedded room also has an en suite bathroom. Both rooms have single rooms adjacent to them for children. At the top of the driveway, an adorable two-bedroom lodge is perfect for families who wish to stay for several days (in summer it is let on a weekly basis). Bruckless is ideally placed for exploring Donegal. *Directions:* From Donegal take the N56 towards Killybegs. The house is on the left in Bruckless village.

BRUCKLESS HOUSE
Owners: Clive & Joan Evans
Bruckless, Co Donegal, Ireland
Tel: (074) 9737071, Fax: (074) 9737070
4 Rooms, Double: €100–€120
1 Cottage: €230–€500 weekly
Open: Apr to Sep, Credit cards: all major
www.karenbrown.com/bruckless.html

This onetime coaching inn was in a sad and sorry state before it was rescued by the present owner, Roy Bolton, and transformed into the delightful hotel you see today. A rocking chair sits before an enormous fireplace and displays of old plates adorn the mantle. The ambiance of an old coaching inn continues to the restaurant with its whitewashed stone walls and tall pine settles dividing the room into intimate little areas. The inn's original kitchen, with its flagstone floor and open fire, links the hotel to the Victorian-style bar still illuminated by flickering gas light. Try a Black Bush whiskey from the distillery up the road—Bushmills is the home of the world's oldest licensed distillery and you can take a tour around it. There is a broad range of bedrooms. The most desirable are definitely the Superior Rooms of the Mill House, where you can expect to be pampered up to best 5-star standards. However, all the Mill House rooms are spacious with a small sitting area and ample room for luggage and golf clubs (lots of excellent courses nearby, including Royal Portrush). Small budget price rooms are also available in the original Coaching Inn overlooking the village. Just up the road are the picturesque ruins of 13th-century Dunluce Castle and the Giant's Causeway. *Directions:* From Coleraine take the B19 to Bushmills. As you cross the River Bush, the main entrance to the hotel is on your left.

BUSHMILLS INN HOTEL
Managers: Stella Minogue & Alan Dunlop
9 Dunluce Road
Bushmills
Co Antrim BT57 8QG, Northern Ireland
Tel: (028) 2073 3000, Fax: (028) 2073 2048
32 Rooms, Double: £98–£248
Dinner: from £30
Open: all year, Credit cards: MC, VS
Ireland Blue Book
www.karenbrown.com/bushmillsinn.html

Craig Park is a perfectly peaceful spot ideally located for visiting Northern Ireland's most famous tourist attraction, the awe-inspiring basalt columns of the Giant's Causeway. Jan and David Cheal lived all over the world (Africa, Australia, Hong Kong, USA, South America) before settling here and they find that welcoming guests from around the world is a way for them to continue to travel. Guests have the entire front of the house, a modern Georgian-style extension to the 18th-century section that the Cheals occupy. There are lots of mementos from the places they have lived, as well as some of their son's sculptures. The hall table is laden with information on where to go and what to see in the area. Spread out your maps in the spacious sitting room and ask David to plot your sightseeing routes. The three bedrooms have several beds so that they can accommodate from two to five guests. All have en suite shower rooms and there's an extra bathroom across the hall for those who prefer a tub. Two gentle Labradors love to romp with children in the grassy garden. Breakfast is the only meal served but there are several places to eat in nearby Bushmills. *Directions:* From Bushmills follow signs to the distillery. Immediately after the distillery, turn left then first right after the Citroen garage. After 1.6 km turn left onto Carnbore Road and Craig Park is signposted to your left.

CRAIG PARK
Owners: Jan & David Cheal
24 Carnbore Road
Bushmills
Co Antrim BT57 8YF, Northern Ireland
Tel: (028) 2073 2496, 3 Rooms, Double: £60–£70
Closed: Christmas & New Year, Credit cards: MC, VS
www.karenbrown.com/craigpark.html

Even though it is only just over 4 kilometers from the Ring of Kerry, Iskeroon is one of the most hidden and secluded properties in Ireland. Reached by a precipitous lane that tumbles down to the sea and a narrow farm track, Iskeroon boasts the most spectacular view in Ireland—truly a hidden gem. Geraldine and David are the first family to call this home, for while the house was built in the '30s, it was previously used as holiday home. Snuggling into a sheltered spot, the long, low-lying house captures the sea view from every room, a view so enchanting that it takes you a while to realize that the house is also delightful with its three spacious bedrooms, living room, and dining room decorated in Mediterranean shades of yellow, blue, red, and green—furnished in a most attractive, unfussy way. Robes are provided for nipping across the hall to your private bathrooms. A lovely, two-person, self-catering apartment is found in the stables. The nearby town of Waterville has a good selection of restaurants for dinner—David and Geraldine are happy to advise. The garden tumbles down to a private jetty. Guests often take the boat from Bunavalla pier to the Skelligs. *Directions:* Derrynane is between Waterville and Caherdaniel. Find the Scarriff Inn (a large red building) between these villages and take the road signposted Bunavalla Pier all the way to the bottom. At the pier turn left over the track beside the beach to Iskeroon.

ISKEROON
Owners: Geraldine & David Hare
Caherdaniel, Derrynane, Co Kerry, Ireland
Tel: (066) 9475119, Fax: (066) 9475488
3 Rooms, Double: €150
1 Apartment: €450–€500 weekly
Open: May to Sep, Credit cards: all major
www.karenbrown.com/iskeroon.html

Lisdonagh House's last owner, Valda Palmer, discouraged visitors and frequently shot at them on sight. Thankfully a very different welcome is offered today by Finola and John Cooke. A smile, warm handshake, and a restorative cup of tea in the drawing room is their standard prescription for those of us who have wandered around seemingly identical lanes looking for the place (though it's certainly worth getting lost to stay here deep in the countryside). A striking feature of the house is the oval entrance hall with its 1790 murals depicting the virtues of valor, chastity, beauty, and justice. This leads to a grand staircase, which arches up to bedrooms and down to further bedrooms and a stone-faced lounge-cum-bar at the base of the tower. The house has been totally restored. Walk down to Lough Hackett and take the rowing boat out to the crannóg, a man-made island reputedly the home of the High Kings of Connaught over 2,000 years ago. Farther afield lie Galway and Cong. Lisdonagh can be rented as a whole on a self-catering basis or complete with chef and housekeeping staff. There are also two Victorian villas which can be rented for the night or on a weekly basis. *Directions:* From the N18 (Galway road) follow signposts for Sligo through Claregalway and keep on the N17 towards Tuam (about 18 km). Turn left on the R333 towards Headford to Caherlistrane. At Quealey's pub turn right towards Shrule and after 2 km turn left to Lisdonagh House.

LISDONAGH HOUSE
Owners: Finola & John Cooke
Caherlistrane, Headford
Co Galway, Ireland
Tel: (093) 31163, Fax: (093) 31528
10 Rooms, Double: €140–€240
2 Cottages: €850–€980 weekly
Dinner: €45
Open: May to Oct, Credit cards: all major
Ireland Blue Book
www.karenbrown.com/lisdonagh.html

Ballaghtobin has everything: a beautifully decorated and furnished interior; acres of scenic parkland with a ruined Norman church just steps from the front door; an excellent location for exploring the Counties of Waterford and Kilkenny; and the most welcoming of owners in Mickey and Catherine Gabbett. Catherine's flair for interior design is evident in every elegant, informal room—soft, warm pastel walls, beautiful paintings, lovely antiques—it's very easy to settle in here. Bedrooms are absolutely gorgeous and have sparkling modern bathrooms. My favorite is the spacious Barrack Room—in years gone by, guests who drank too much at parties were sent here to sleep. Breakfast is the only meal served and for dinner guests often go to the Hunter Yard at Mount Juliet. You could really spend a week doing something totally different each day. There is medieval Kilkenny city with its wealth of historical sights; the craft trail that combines potters, leather makers, and glass blowers; golf courses from local to championship; Waterford with its historic harbor and famous crystal; and Cashel with its rock and historic abbey. *Directions:* From the main crossroads in the center of Callan take the road signed "Callan Garden Centre" (Mill Street). Go straight for 5 km (past Callan golf Club) and follow a sharp bend to the left. Take the left fork at the Y-junction (house is signposted) and after about .5 km Ballaghtobin's entrance is on your left opposite a pink gate lodge.

BALLAGHTOBIN
Owners: Catherine & Mickey Gabbett
Callan, Co Kilkenny, Ireland
Tel: (056) 7725227, Fax: (056) 7725712
3 Rooms, Double: €100
Closed: Dec & Jan, Credit cards: MC, VS
www.karenbrown.com/ballaghtobin.html

This is the place to stay if you are a garden buff for this lovely Georgian house, built in 1794, is surrounded by 7 acres of glorious gardens. Started in 1947, the gardens extend from walled formality with trim lawns and herbaceous borders to a magical informal woodland garden complete with millpond and literary corner where you can curl up with a good book. It's home to Mark and Emma Hewlett and their three young boys who Emma fervently hopes will be keen gardeners too. It's a lovely place to base yourself for explorations along the southeast coast. An ideal place to relax and enjoy the spectacular gardens, tennis court, heated indoor pool, exercise room or indulge yourself with a massage and aromatherapy session. Dinner in the peacock dining room is a real treat there's always fresh fish on the menu and most of the vegetables and fruit comes from the extensive kitchen garden. Breakfast and lunch are enjoyed in the airy conservatory which doubles as the Pink Teacup café for daytime garden visitors. Two interconnecting courtyard bedrooms are especially handy for families and friends traveling together. In the house Magnolia is an particularly inviting room with its large four-poster bed and clawfoot-tub with garden view. The Coach House and the Garden Suite are two lovely, self-catering apartments. *Directions:* From New Ross take the R733 signposted Campile and follow signposts to Kilmokea Gardens.

KILMOKEA
Owners: Emma & Mark Hewlett
Campile, Great Island, Co Wexford, Ireland
Tel: (051) 388109, Fax: (051) 388766
6 Rooms, Double: €160–€280
2 Apartments: €650–€950 weekly
Dinner: from €45-€50
Open: Feb to Oct, Credit cards: MC, VS
Hidden Ireland
www.karenbrown.com/kilmokea.html

Paul's parents bought this huge home when he was a child and quickly discovered that it was far too large to maintain as a family home without an army of staff, so they opened it up to guests. His mum, Jean, while claiming to be retired still enthusiastically advises guests on where to go and what to see between breakfast and dinner—she has enough sightseeing venues to occupy a fortnight. Wife Clare does the front of house in an evening while Paul is in the kitchen. Up the grand staircase there are some very spacious, well equipped and comfortable bedrooms—be sure to discuss the size of bed, several are large zip-and-link beds while others are smaller with lovely old head and footboards. Do not miss the opportunity to visit Lismore Castle, Swiss Cottage, and Waterford Crystal, or to take a drive over The Vee. You need to keep busy to work off the delicious dinners that Paul prepares (a set four-course menu with choices or the flexibility of being able to order à la carte). Old and new guests alike revel in the relaxed idiosyncrasy of the place. *Directions:* From Waterford take the N72 (Killarney road) for about a one-hour drive to Cappoquin. Richmond House is on the left just before you enter town.

RICHMOND HOUSE
Owner: The Deevy family
Cappoquin, Co Waterford, Ireland
Tel: (058) 54278, Fax: (058) 54988
9 Rooms, Double: €160–€240
Dinner: €50 (not Sun)
Open: Feb to Dec, Credit cards: all major
www.karenbrown.com/richmond.html

Hollywell is set in a large garden overlooking the River Shannon. It has a secluded riverside location, just a couple of minutes' walk to the heart of Carrick-on-Shannon, a lively riverside town. Tom and Rosaleen provide outstanding hospitality in their lovely old home. Guests have a large sitting room with comfy sofas, books, games, and TV where they gather round the fire in the evening. Breakfast is the only meal served at the little tables arranged round the grand piano in the dining room, but for dinner guests often go to the Oarsman on Bridge Street run by sons Conor and Ronan. Three grandfather clocks grace the hallways and a sofa and books are grouped at the head of the stairs to take advantage of the view over a broad stretch of the river. The two very large front bedrooms share the same lovely view, while the back bedrooms are small only in comparison to those at the front. You can fish without ever leaving Hollywell's grounds and there's an 18-hole golf club nearby. A few of the stately houses within reach are Strokestown House and Gardens, Carriglass, Clonalis, King House, Florence Court, Castle Coole, and Belvedere House and Gardens. Ask about the possibility of renting a launch for a day and take a little meander up the River Shannon. *Directions:* From Dublin take the N4 (Sligo road) to Carrick. Cross the river, turn up the hill by Gings pub, and Hollywell is on the left.

HOLLYWELL
Owners: Rosaleen & Tom Maher
Liberty Hill
Carrick-on-Shannon
Co Leitrim, Ireland
Tel & Fax: (071) 96 21124
4 Rooms, Double: €110–€140
Closed: Christmas & New Year, Credit cards: all major
www.karenbrown.com/hollywell.html

The setting for Cashel House is spectacularly impressive: at the head of Cashel Bay with Cashel Hill standing guard behind, a solid white house nestles amongst acres and acres of woodland and gardens of exotic flowering shrubs. Kilometers of garden footpaths are yours to wander along, and the beautiful seashore is yours to explore. This is not the kind of hotel to spend just a night in—once you have settled into your lovely room and sampled the exquisite food in the splendid conservatory dining room, you will be glad that you have made Cashel House the base for your Connemara explorations. Graceful antiques, turf fires, and lovely arrangements of freshly picked flowers create a warm, country-house welcome. It feels particularly decadent to have breakfast served to you in bed on a prettily decorated tray. All the bedrooms are beautifully furnished and decorated, each accompanied by a sparkling bathroom. Thirteen exquisite suites occupy a wing and enjoy comfortable sitting areas overlooking the garden. Tennis rackets are available so that keen tennis players can enjoy the court bordering the bay. Just down the road a small two bedroom cottage, with bay views, is let on a weekly basis. *Directions:* Take the N59 from Galway (towards Clifden) through Oughterard and turn left to the village of Cashel 2 km after Recess.

CASHEL HOUSE
Owners: Kay & Dermot McEvilly
Cashel, Co Galway, Ireland
Tel: (095) 31001, Fax: (095) 31077
32 Rooms, Double: €170–€310*
1 Cottage: €600 weekly
Service: 12.5%
Dinner: from €50
Closed: mid-Jan to mid-Feb, Credit cards: all major
Relais & Châteaux, Ireland Blue Book
www.karenbrown.com/cashelhouse.html

An excellent location and a warm welcome from hosts Grazielle and John Quinlan combine to make Legends Townhouse a winner. The Rock of Cashel looms large behind the house and imposing views of the rocky outcrop topped with its cluster of ancient buildings are to be enjoyed from the restaurant, one of the sitting areas, and several of the bedrooms. The house was purpose-built by a former owner who was not concerned with architectural merit. However, once you are inside, lots of country pine, simple but pleasing decor, and Grazielle and John's tender care, make up for the architecture. Traditional Irish fare is served for breakfast and dinner in the dining room. From mid-June to mid-September book dinner for 7 pm so that you can dine in time to head through the back garden and adjacent car park to the theater to enjoy a toe-tapping evening of "Brú Ború"—traditional Irish dancing and music. Grazielle will happily make reservations for you. The town itself deserves a day for sightseeing and shopping, but Legends also makes an excellent base for exploring Kilkenny, Waterford, and Cahir Castle, coming home each night in plenty of time for dinner. *Directions:* Arriving from Dublin on the N8, you see an Esso garage on the right on the outskirts of town. Twenty meters beyond, turn right and do a U-turn onto the R660 towards Holycross. Legends Townhouse is 20 meters down this road on the left.

LEGENDS TOWNHOUSE & RESTAURANT
Owners: Grazielle & John Quinlan
Cashel, Co Tipperary, Ireland
Tel: (062) 61292, Fax: none
7 Rooms, Double: €110–€130
Dinner: €40 (not Wed)
Open: all year, Credit cards: MC, VS
www.karenbrown.com/legends.html

Ballyvolane is a great Irish country house. Set a few miles from Fermoy it's a perfect place for sightseeing between Waterford and Kinsale, Cashel to Lismore. It is beautiful at night when the long mahogany table is set with flickering candles and you enjoy drinks by the fire in the grand pillared hallway. It is lovely on a warm morning as you wander through the gardens or whack some croquet balls on the lawn. It's one of those houses that makes you feel happy just thinking about having stayed there. It's a friendly house where guests wander in and out of the kitchen, a vast tall-ceilinged room that was once a drawing room. It is welcoming because Justin and Jenny Green suffuse it with their young energy, their charm and friendliness. Bedrooms are roomy, stylish and furnished with antiques. One has a bath so deep that you have to step up to get into it. Within a radius of a few kilometers there are 20 golf courses and within an hour's drive are Blarney with its famous castle, Cork city, and the bustling boating town of Kinsale. Ballyvolane has seven kilometers of privately managed salmon fishing on the renowned River Blackwater. A self-catering cottage is also available. *Directions:* From Fermoy take the N8 towards Cork to Rathcormac, and Ballyvolane House is 6 km further on down a signposted country lane.

BALLYVOLANE HOUSE
Owners: Jenny & Justin Green
Castlelyons, Co Cork, Ireland
Tel: (025) 36349, Fax: (025) 36781
6 Rooms, Double: €170–€200
1 Cottage: €340–€490 weekly
Dinner: €50
Open: all year, Credit cards: all major
Hidden Ireland
www.karenbrown.com/ballyvolanehouse.html

I'm impressed that Pyers O'Connor Nash's home is built on land that has belonged to his family for over 2,000 years, the ancestral home of the O'Conors of Connaught, descendants of the last High Kings of Ireland and traditional Kings of Connaught. And what a home it is, a grand 45-room Victorian Italianate mansion full of fascinating heirlooms and lovely antique furnishings. There's the coronation stone of the Kings of Connaught by the front door, Carolan's harp, rare manuscripts, and a vast array of family portraits. It could be daunting, but Pyer's and Marguerite's way of sharing their home makes it entrancing: the tremendous dining room with its Sheffield silver from the Great Exhibition, the wondrous array of books in the library, the elegant drawing room. I loved room 13, huge with its historic four-poster bed, fabulous views, and large bathroom with bath and shower; but opted for the green room, my favorite, with its tall four-poster bed and large bathroom. The former billiard room displays interesting manuscripts, and there's a small museum of lace and costumes. When the house is open to the public (June to August) guests are welcome to tag along on the 4 pm tour. On the grounds are three cottages let on a weekly, self-catering basis. Galway and Sligo are an hours drive away. *Directions:* Clonalis House is situated on the west side of Castlerea on N60.

CLONALIS HOUSE
Owners: Marguerite & Pyers O'Connor Nash
Castlerea, Ireland
Tel & Fax: (094) 962 0014
4 Rooms, Double: €180
3 Cottages: €320–€550 weekly
Dinner: €44 (not Sun or Mon)
Open: mid-Apr to Sept, Credit cards: MC, VS
Hidden Ireland
www.karenbrown.com/clonalis.html

Byrne's Mal Dua House is a purpose-built guesthouse just outside Clifden. The sunny lobby doubles as a sitting room with sofas and chairs in deep-pink velour, which match the carpet and the balloon shades. An additional larger sitting room is decorated in shades of pink like the adjacent spacious dining room. All bedrooms are spacious and come with different combinations of double and single beds. All have a bath or shower, hairdryer, TV, phone, trouser press, excellent reading lights, and tea- and coffee-makings. The decor is very attractive, with pastel-painted walls and coordinating drapes and bedspreads. Enjoy dinner in the award-winning Fuchsia Restaurant or just relax in the landscaped gardens. Having spent many years in the United States, Aideen and Peter are very in tune with American taste. An obligatory service charge of 10% is added to your bill. During the third week in August, Clifden hosts the Connemara Pony Show and rooms are at a premium. *Directions:* Take the N59 from Galway to the outskirts of Clifden. Mal Dua is on your right as you enter the town.

BYRNE MAL DUA HOUSE
Owners: Peter & Aideen Byrne
Galway Road
Clifden, Connemara
Co Galway, Ireland
Tel: (095) 21171, Fax: (095) 21739
14 Rooms, Double: €90–€150
Dinner: €38
Open: all year, Credit cards: all major
www.karenbrown.com/maldua.html

On a sunny day there is nowhere more magical than Dolphin Beach House, set on its own 35-acre headland at the head of Clifden Bay. The views across the water to Slyne Head and Ballconneely Bay are the best that wild, untamed places can supply. Billy and Barbara tell me that their headland offers views of dolphins, seals, otters, foxes, and all kinds of seabirds. The view changes by the minute with the vagaries of the Irish weather and you can sit for hours just watching the seascape unfold. Warm weather finds guests soaking up the sun on the most private of beaches. The house was built to give views not only from the dining room but also from several of the bedrooms—be sure to request one of these. I particularly enjoyed Bay View, a tall-ceilinged room with wooden floors, a king-sized sleigh bed, and French windows framing sea views. As well as telling exuberant tales about the area, Billy turns his hand to cooking and offers a set, three-course dinner. It's very much a family operation and when I visited, three of the Foyles' five children were working alongside their parents. *Directions:* Take the N59 from Galway to Clifden and follow the one-way system to the top of town where you take the upper fork at the Y-junction (in front of the Alcock and Brown hotel) onto the Sky Road, which traces the peninsula. After 3 km take the first left for 1 km to Dolphin Beach House.

DOLPHIN BEACH HOUSE
Owners: Barbara & Billy Foyle
Lower Sky Road
Clifden, Connemara
Co Galway, Ireland
Tel: (095) 21204, Fax: (095) 22935
Toll Free: (888) 497-4138 USA
8 Rooms, Double: €150–€190
Dinner: €43
Open: all year, Credit cards: MC, VS
www.karenbrown.com/dolphin.html

The harbormaster certainly picked a pretty site for his home on the quay, with its wide vista of the inlet of Ardbear Bay and the town of Clifden winding up the hillside. Since 1820, Quay House has served variously as the harbormaster's home, a convent, a monastery, and a hotel. Julia and Paddy bought the house and the adjacent cottages in almost derelict condition, giving them a new lease of life as a stylish hotel. They decorated the whole in a refreshingly eclectic style; blending old, modern, and unconventional in an idiosyncratic way with little jokes and quirks such as Vegetarian Alley, a corridor of hunting trophies. Breakfast in the conservatory is the only meal served. For dinner, a five-minute walk brings you into town where there are several good restaurants. There are seven spacious studios, of which six have small fitted kitchens and balconies, and seven bedrooms. All rooms have spacious bathrooms with separate showers and tubs. Several are "traditional country house" in their decor, others light, fresh, and more bohemian. Particular favorites are Napoleon, a tribute room to the famous Corsican; Out of Africa, a safari-themed studio; and The Bird Room, a studio with a few wacky stuffed parrots and a couple of large pictures featuring parrots. *Directions:* Take the N59 from Galway to Clifden and follow the one-way system to the top of the town where you take the lower fork at the first Y-junction down onto the quay.

THE QUAY HOUSE
Owners: Julia & Paddy Foyle
Beach Road
Clifden, Connemara
Co Galway, Ireland
Tel: (095) 21369, Fax: (095) 21608
14 Rooms, Double: €130–€170
Open: mid-Mar to Nov, Credit cards: MC, VS
Hidden Ireland
www.karenbrown.com/quayhouse.html

How fortuitous that the storm of Christmas 1998 ripped off SeaMist's roof and caused such damage that only one room was habitable! This catapulted Sheila and her twin sister, whom she was visiting in California, into deciding to completely renovate this lovely old home with Sheila running it as a bed and breakfast. With her easy, friendly manner (not to mention talent at baking and jam-making), Sheila has proved a natural for the job. Add to this SeaMist's central location in Clifden and we have a real winner. Bedrooms are on the whole very spacious and accompanied by either a large bathroom or smaller shower room. Red-deal plank floors complement the warm pastel decor. For a sort of sea view, request a room at the top of the house and you'll catch a glimpse by standing on your tiptoes. Sheila's granddad was an auctioneer and some of his purchases have stayed at the house. I particularly admired the grand sideboard in the sitting room and the beautiful tall pine dresser purchased from Ballynahinch Castle. Walk out the front door and you are steps away from the main street of town with its shops, restaurants, and pubs. Drive a few yards in the other direction and you are in the lovely Connemara countryside. *Directions:* Take the N59 from Galway to Clifden and follow the one-way system to the top of town. Take a left at the square with the Alcock and Brown Hotel to the right. SeaMist is immediately on your right.

SEAMIST
Owner: Sheila Griffin
Clifden, Connemara, Co Galway, Ireland
Tel: (095) 21441, Fax: none
6 Rooms, Double: €70–€110
Closed: midweek in winter, Credit cards: MC, VS
www.karenbrown.com/seaview.html

If you long to visit a spot off the beaten track and enjoy wonderful hospitality and divine food, you can do no better than to stay with Lucy and Johnny Madden on the Hilton Park estate. Lucy's passion is growing vegetables for the kitchen and Johnny's family home is so grand that it is hard to believe that it is a real home and not the kind where you pay a visitor's entrance fee. It's a beautiful house of lovely rooms where guestrooms range from vast (the gorgeous Blue room and Parents room) with grand floor-to-ceiling beds that you climb into, views of the lake and large bathrooms with claw-foot tubs, to more modest in size, with regular-sized bathrooms containing old soaking tubs. Guests relax in the beautiful drawing room, enjoying pre-dinner drinks, conversation, and views across the terrace of formal gardens to the lake. The same enchanting view is enjoyed in the elegant dining room where guests dine at separate tables by the gentle flicker of candlelight. Breakfast is taken "below stairs" in the former servants' hall. Have your own house party by renting the entire place. Popular sightseeing includes Belleek with its pottery, Lough Erne, Castle Coole (a restored Palladian mansion), and Florence Court (a riot of rococo plasterwork). *Directions:* From the Cavan by-pass take the turnoff for Ballyhaise. Go through Ballyhaise and Scotshouse and the entrance to Hilton Park is on your left 1 km after the golf course.

HILTON PARK
Owners: Lucy & Johnny Madden
Clones, Scotshouse, Co Monaghan, Ireland
Tel: (047) 56007, Fax: (047) 56033
6 Rooms, Double: €250–€300
Dinner: €52 (not Sun or Mon)
Open: all year, Credit cards: MC, VS
Hidden Ireland
www.karenbrown.com/hilton.html

Guests stopping at Rockwood House on their way north have been known to go no farther, contenting themselves with whiling away the hours in this peaceful spot and enjoying the warm hospitality that Susan and James McCauley offer. Susan and James returned here after living in Dublin for many years, acquired a derelict rectory with trees growing through the roof, and replaced it with a well-appointed replica-Rockwood House. Enjoy breakfast in the conservatory overlooking the garden or just relax around the fire in the guests sitting room. For dinner guests often go to the Derragarra Inn just down the road in Butlersbridge or, for fancier fare, the nearby Olde Post Restaurant. Upstairs, the spacious, very nicely decorated bedrooms are each accompanied by a snug bathroom. Beds are double, twin, or king if you request that the twin beds be zipped together. County Cavan is blessed with picture-postcard scenery—whichever way you turn you find waterways, rivers, and lakes set among gently rolling hills. Opportunities for fishing and walking abound. Popular sightseeing includes Belleek, with its pottery, Lough Erne, Castle Coole (a restored Palladian mansion), and Florence Court (a riot of rococo plaster). *Directions:* From Cavan follow signs for the N3 to Monaghan, then turn right at the sign for Monaghan/Butlersbridge (N54). Rockwood House is on your left, 3 km from the village of Butlersbridge.

ROCKWOOD HOUSE
Owners: Susan & James McCauley
Cloverhill, Belturbet, Co Cavan, Ireland
Tel: (047) 55351, Fax: (047) 55373
4 Rooms, Double: €64
Closed: Dec 10 to Feb 1, Credit cards: MC, VS
www.karenbrown.com/rockwood.html

Set high above the river surrounded by over three acres of grounds this grand 1840s Victorian commands an impressive position in Cobh—but the main point of interest is the fabulous interior as Pam and John spared no expense in revamping their longtime home into luxury guest accommodation. Their easy hospitality, as much as the comfort of their lovely home, is what makes Knockeven House special. Your stay often begins with tea and scones by the drawing room fire. Up the grand curving staircase you find the airy bedrooms—two have six foot beds (can also be twin), one has a queen, and the fourth has an adorable double bed (historic half tester) and gorgeous silk drapes. Showers are large, bedrooms are wired for internet access, and TVs are available. Scrambled eggs and smoked salmon is a breakfast specialty. Favorite activities are visiting Cobh's cathedral, taking the ferry to Kinsale, going to Blarney to kiss the famous stone, and visiting the English market and shops in nearby Cork. John, an avid golfer, is a mine of information on local courses and happy to arranges tee times. *Directions:* Just before you arrive in Cork (from N25—Waterford to Cork Road) turn left on R624 to Cobh. On entering Cobh, pass the ferry on your right. At Satoil garage take a sharp left and an immediate right into the Knockeven House's driveway.

KNOCKEVEN HOUSE
Owners: Pam & John Mulhaire
Rushbrooke
Cobh, Co Cork, Ireland
Tel: (021) 4811778, Fax: (021) 4811719
4 Rooms, Double: €120–€130
Open: all year, Credit cards: MC, VS
www.karenbrown.com/knockeven.html

The charm of Greenhill House is Elizabeth Hegarty, who is exceptionally sweet and helpful. I very much enjoyed the late-evening conversation around the drawing room fire sharing tea and cakes with James and Elizabeth and fellow guests. All this after tea, cake and conversation upon arrival. Elizabeth and James are very knowledgeable about the area and happy to direct guests on where to go and what to see—of course the nearby Antrim coast is particularly popular. The farmhouse is delightfully old-fashioned and lovingly decorated with antiques, with bouquets of fresh garden flowers adding the finishing touch. Our bedroom (overlooking the garden) had everything: sightseeing information; a tray set with teapot, kettle, tea bags, coffee, and chocolate; hairdryer; television; and even a little box of After Eight mints by the bedside. Plump comforters top the beds and fluffy towels hang on the old-fashioned towel rail. Bedrooms in the attic have bathrooms tucked neatly under the eaves while other rooms have snug shower rooms, in what at first appears to be large fitted closets. A bountiful breakfast is the only meal served. *Directions:* From Limavady take the A37 towards Coleraine, turn right on the A29 (Garvagh and Cookstown road) for 11 km. Turn left on the B66 (Greenhill Road) and Greenhill House is on the right.

GREENHILL HOUSE
Owners: Elizabeth & James Hegarty
24 Greenhill Road
Coleraine, Aghadowey
Co Londonderry BT51 4EU, Northern Ireland
Tel: (028) 7086 8241, Fax: (028) 7086 8365
6 Rooms, Double: £60
Open: Mar to Oct, Credit cards: MC, VS
www.karenbrown.com/greenhill.html

Mary and Declan Kelleher like nothing more than to share their love of the Burren with visitors. They have gone so far as to compile a most interesting booklet on the district, which details its history and points of interest. To make sure you do not go wrong they will kit you out with maps and instructions on what to do each day. Fergus View was built as a teacher's residence at the turn of the last century and Declan's grandfather was its first occupant. Continuing in his grandfather's footsteps, Declan is the principal of Corofin's primary school. The next generation of teachers is in place with several of Mary and Declan's children training to be teachers. In an evening the fire is lit in the little parlor to encourage you to make yourself at home. A hearty breakfast is the only meal served but handily there's a restaurant in the village for dinner. Bedrooms are prettily decorated with matching drapes and bedspreads. All are of the leave-large-cases-in-the-car variety—facilities are not designed for persons of large proportions. The Kellehers also have a lovely self-catering cottage for week-long stays. The nearby Burren is fascinating, and the Cliffs of Moher are close at hand. *Directions:* From Shannon airport take the N18 to Ennis, the N85 towards Lisdoonvarna, turn first right to Corofin, go through the village, and the house is on your left after 3 km.

FERGUS VIEW
Owners: Mary & Declan Kelleher
Corofin, Kilnaboy, Co Clare, Ireland
Tel: (065) 6837606, Fax: (065) 6837192
6 Rooms, Double: €70–€74
1 Cottage: €630 weekly
Open: mid Mar to mid-Oct, Credit cards: none
www.karenbrown.com/fergusview.html

St. Clerans has had an impressive list of Irish owners but came into the limelight when John Huston (film director extraordinaire) called it home for over 20 years and spent an absolute mint on the place. More recently this impressive home prepared itself for the 21st century with another no-holds-barred face-lift from its current owner, former chat-show host Merv Griffin, and when he is not in residence you can enjoy a stay at his luxurious retreat. It's a treat to see an architectural gem coddled to the extent where everything is the absolute best that money can buy—the essence of pure indulgence. My personal favorite room is Merv's suite—you can unpack into his very own closet and admire the artwork that Merv has places in the niches that once held John Houston's Oscars. The most private bedroom is the octagonal little building that was once Angelica Huston's playhouse. She would not recognize it today with its stenciled walls and opulent bathroom. Spend the day lounging on the premises soaking up the ambiance and being totally spoiled by the attentive Irish staff, play golf at Athenry and Loughrea, or go horseriding or clay pigeon shooting. The cliffs of Moher on the Burren and Galway city are within easy striking distance. *Directions:* From Galway take the N6 towards Dublin for 30 km to Craughwell. Go through the village and take the second left signposted St. Clerans and Athenry for the 8-km drive to St. Clerans.

ST. CLERANS
Owner: Merv Griffin
Craughwell, Co Galway, Ireland
Tel: (091) 846555, Fax: (091) 846752
12 Rooms, Double: €325–€525
Dinner: €65 (not Mon)
Open: all year when Merv's not there
Credit cards: all major
www.karenbrown.com/stclerans.html

Enniscoe House is the home of Susan Kellett—a descendant of the original family who settled this estate in the 1670s—her son DJ, and their Labrador Frodo. Staying as her guest gives you a glimpse of what it was like to live in a grand country mansion—the old family furniture, portraits, books, and family memorabilia are yours to enjoy. The lofty rooms are decorated true to the Georgian period and all are in tiptop condition. The three front bedrooms, of grand proportions, are reached by a grand elliptical staircase. Those in the older part of the house are less grand but just as lovely. I particularly enjoyed the old nursery with half-tester and twin beds, and comfortable chintz chairs. Dinners by soft, flickering candlelight at little tables in the large dining room are a real treat. Tucked behind the house, the courtyard buildings house three delightful farmhouse-style self-catering apartments. The Victorian walled garden has been given a new lease of life and the barns display old farm machinery and artifacts. Fishery manager Barry Segrave offers help to anglers fishing Lough Conn (tel: 096-31853, fax: 096-31773). Walk the trails that go through the woodlands past the forestry plantations and along the lake shore. There are great cliffs along the north coast, where the Stone-Age settlements at Céide Fields have been excavated. *Directions:* From Ballina take the N59 to Crossmolina, turn left in town for Castlebar, and the house is on the left after 3 km.

ENNISCOE HOUSE
Owners: Susan & DJ Kellett
Castlehill
Crossmolina, Co Mayo, Ireland
Tel: (096) 31112, Fax: (096) 31773
6 Rooms, Double: €178–€230
3 Cottages: €600–€750 weekly
Dinner: €50
Open: Apr to mid-Oct, Credit cards: MC, VS
Hidden Ireland
www.karenbrown.com/enniscoehouse.html

Doyle's Restaurant, owned and run by John, Charlotte and Clodagh Clusky, is famous the world over for the excellence of its seafood, fresh from the ocean. A small village shop and pub built in 1790 house the welcoming restaurant with its flagstone floor and cozy arrangements of tables and chairs, while the house next door offers the most delightful accommodation in Dingle. The two houses are interconnected yet self-contained, so that guests can come and go to the restaurant but will not have their peace disturbed when they are sleeping. You step from the street into the old-fashioned parlor with its pine floor, grandfather clock, and sofas drawn into seating areas. Large umbrellas are close at hand in case you should need them. The top-notch bedrooms have excellent bathrooms equipped with everything you might need. The two ground-floor rooms are ideal for anyone who has difficulty with stairs. After dinner inquire at the bar which of the many little pubs has traditional music that night and stroll along to join in the merriment. *Directions:* Dingle is a 2½-hour drive from Limerick. Turn right at the roundabout, right into John Street, and Doyle's is on your left.

DOYLE'S
Owners: John, Charlotte & Clodagh Clusky
John Street
Dingle, Co Kerry, Ireland
Tel: (066) 9151174, Fax: (066) 9151816
8 Rooms, Double: €95–€160
Dinner: à la carte (not Sun)
Closed: mid-Jan to mid-Feb, Credit cards: all major
www.karenbrown.com/doyles.html

Mary and John Curran are locals who built Greenmount House as a home for themselves and their small children then later cleverly expanded their bungalow adding a large sitting room, additional family accommodation, and large top-of-the-line guestrooms. Seven face the harbor and six have either French windows opening onto a patio or balcony (chairs provided for sitting out) and are large enough to accommodate a spacious sitting area—the kind of rooms you want to spend time in. Drift into the view in room 6 (Garran) whose bed and sofa face a breathtaking vista of Connor Pass soaring above the fields. A conservatory breakfast room, prettily furnished with painted pine furniture, has a panoramic view across fields and Dingle's rooftops to the harbor. Mary prepares the most bountiful of breakfasts and tries to offer at least two fruit dishes, delicious mueslis, and yogurts, as well as a cooked breakfast menu that includes not only the traditional breakfast but also fish and mushrooms in yogurt sauce. Breakfast is the only meal served. For dinner stroll down the hill into town where there are some particularly fine fish restaurants. Wander down to the harbor and watch the catch come in, window shop, and enjoy a pint in one of the many pubs. *Directions:* Turn right at the roundabout in Dingle, next right into John Street, and continue up the hill to Greenmount House.

GREENMOUNT HOUSE
Owners: Mary & John Curran
Gortonora
Dingle, Co Kerry, Ireland
Tel: (066) 9151414, Fax: (066) 9151974
9 Rooms, Double: €100–€170
Closed: Christmas, Credit cards: MC, VS
www.karenbrown.com/greenmounthouse.html

Heaton's, a purpose-built guesthouse, commands an enviable position at the head of Dingle Bay, with spectacular views across the water to Burnham Headlands. The mouth of the sheltered harbor is just a five-minute walk from the heart of this lively town. While the style outside is modern, the inside is more traditional with classic French furniture. The bedrooms are smartly decorated with beds coming in sizes from twin to king. Nuala is a stickler for quality when it comes to bedding and towels, so crisp white sheets adorn the beds and good-quality towels hang in the sparkling white bathrooms, which all have power showers over the tubs. Ten of the rooms have views to the bay and three are large enough to accommodate a second bed for a child (request a second-floor room for the best view). Rooms 14 and 16 are the most spacious of rooms, with a king-sized bed, roomy sitting area, and Jacuzzi tub and shower. Daughter Jackie, the breakfast chef, makes certain breakfast is a full Irish spread of local produce, with the fish and omelettes, made with free-range eggs, deserving a special mention. *Directions:* Arriving in Dingle, keep the harbor to your left and Heaton's is located 600 yards beyond the marina on your right, overlooking the bay.

HEATON'S
Owners: Nuala, Jackie & Cameron Heaton
The Wood
Dingle, Co Kerry, Ireland
Tel: (066) 9152288, Fax: (066) 9152324
16 Rooms, Double: €132–€180
Open: all year, Credit cards: MC, VS
www.karenbrown.com/heatons.html

Set on a wooded, tidal island in Donegal Bay and joined to the mainland by a narrow causeway, St. Ernan's House was built in 1826 by John Hamilton, a nephew of the Duke of Wellington, for his wife. Over lunch here one day, Brian and Carmel O'Dowd decided that St. Ernan's was the kind of hotel they would like to own, so several years later when it came on the market they took the plunge and forsook their careers in banking and teaching to become hoteliers. From almost every one of the rooms you are treated to marvelous views across a mirrorlike span of water. In the lounge, window seats offer views across the water to the mainland and chairs are artfully arranged to provide numerous nooks for intimate after-dinner conversation. A four-course candlelit dinner, with choices for each course, is served in the dining room. The attractive bedrooms come in all shapes and sizes, and while almost all have delightful water views, the largest command the highest prices. Be sure to enjoy the walk around this delightful little island. You'll find some excellent shops in Donegal town, amongst them Magees, famous for its tweed. Beyond Donegal town lies the wild, rugged landscape that has made this county famous. *Directions:* From Sligo take the N15 towards Donegal as far as the village of Laghey (6.5 km before Donegal). Approximately 1.5 km past Laghey take the left-hand turn onto R267. Proceed for 1.6 km and St. Ernan's is signposted to your left.

ST. ERNAN'S HOUSE
Owners: Carmel & Brian O'Dowd
Donegal, Co Donegal, Ireland
Tel: (07497) 21065, Fax: (07497) 22098
10 Rooms, Double: €230–€360
Dinner: €50 (on Tues, Fri and Sat only)
Open: mid-Apr to Oct, Credit cards: MC, VS
Ireland Blue Book
www.karenbrown.com/sternans.html

"What a great place to have a party!" I exclaimed—and the thought had not escaped former owners, for there are tales in the town of grand parties long ago with guests dancing in the expansive drawing and dining rooms and a quartet in the back hallway. These aristocratic rooms have been restored to their former glory, with a wedding-cake icing of plasterwork ringing their lofty ceilings above sink-in sofas and chairs and a vast dining-room table. Upstairs has received the same sensitive treatment. The two premier rooms at the front of the house have vast bathrooms with large tubs and separate showers and enough room in the bedrooms to accommodate seating by the fire and a couple of beds. Between them stands an extra bedroom (without bath), ideal for an older child or traveling companion. The fourth bedroom overlooks the courtyard. For dinner guests usually drive to local restaurants. With advance notice Laura will prepare supper. Michael and Laura find that many guests are interested in their restoration and often give a tour of "behind the scenes" portions of the property. *Directions:* From Mallow take the N20 towards Limerick for 6.5 km to New Twopothouse. Turn right for the 6.5-km drive to Doneraile where you find Creagh House on your left at the far end of the main street.

CREAGH HOUSE
Owners: Laura O'Mahony & Michael O'Sullivan
Main Street
Doneraile, Co Cork, Ireland
Tel: (022) 24433, Fax: (022) 24715
4 Rooms, Double: €160
Supper: €25
Open: Mar to Oct, Credit cards: all major
Hidden Ireland
www.karenbrown.com/creagh.html

Isolated by acres of fields and gardens, Belcamp Hutchinson is an oasis of country house elegance just 7 minutes' drive from Dublin airport. It is such an outstanding home and Doreen is such a gracious hostess that you will want to stay for several days and make this your base for Dublin and the surrounding area. On arrival you'll doubtless be greeted by the dogs, Bullseye, and Dusty, who love to meet guests. A fire is lit in the drawing room in the evening; relax, help yourself to a drink from the honor bar and make yourself at home. There's also a little TV room with "all" the channels—on the night I stayed guests were watching a sports match—however you also have a TV with local channels in your bedroom. Up the elegant staircase, spacious bedrooms are decorated in strong, dark, Georgian colors, each beautifully coordinated with lovely fabrics. Three further rooms are located atop the house with Gold being a particularly fun one. Large beds are the order of the day and there's always candies and interesting magazines by the bedside. Breakfast is a real treat with ham, an array of cheeses, fruit, cereal and yogurt in addition to a cooked breakfast. Be sure to explore the walled garden—the maze is a fun challenge. Leave your car and take the bus for the 30-minute ride to the heart of Dublin. *Directions:* Belcamp Hutchinson is just off the Malahide Road in Balgriffin. Doreen will fax or mail you detailed directions. See Dublin Walking Tour map for location.

BELCAMP HUTCHINSON
Owners: Doreen Gleson & Karl Waldburg
Carrs Lane, Malahide Road
Dublin, Balgriffin, Ireland
Tel: (01) 846 0843, Fax: (01) 848 5703
8 Rooms, Double: €150
Closed: Christmas, Credit cards: MC, VS
www.karenbrown.com/belcamphutchinson.html

The heart of Temple Bar with its trendy stores and vibrant nightlife is a most appropriate spot for a luxury boutique hotel. Originally built in 1852, the building was for many years a cleric's residence. The conversion to a hotel kept all the attractive architectural features such as oak paneling, wooden floors, and lovely old windows. The cleric colors of purple, brown, red, blue, and gold are subtly included in every room. Decor is uncluttered, with simple lines. Relax in the peace and quiet of the study with its open fire, writing table, and wood-paneled walls or join the hubbub of the Octagon Bar with its crowded little alcoves. The Tea Room is one of the most lauded restaurants in the country. Bedrooms are decorated in natural tones and muted colors—all very serene—and double glazing ensures a quiet night's sleep. The handcrafted beds are king sized and rooms are equipped with interactive TV, entertainment systems, and high-speed internet access. The location, overlooking the River Liffey on Dublin's "left bank" is perfect for exploring Dublin on foot. The hotel has a small garage and valet parking is available. *Directions:* Wellington Quay is on the south bank of the River Liffey—see Dublin Walking Tour map for location.

THE CLARENCE
Manager: Olivier Sevestre
6–8 Wellington Quay
Dublin, Ireland
Tel: (01) 407 0800, Fax: (01) 407 0820
49 Rooms, Double: €340–€2500*
*Breakfast not included: €27.5
Dinner: €55
Closed: Christmas, Credit cards: all major
www.karenbrown.com/clarence.html

Just steps from St. Stephen's Green in the heart of Georgian Dublin, Harrington Hall is ideally located for walking to all the city's attractions. The tranquility of the spacious sitting room with its gold brocade sofas and comfortable armchairs drawn round a welcoming peat fire quickly convinced me that this was an enticing place to stay in central Dublin. Handsome Henry, who runs the hotel with his parents Monica and Joe, has taken great care with the design of the bedrooms—their size, amenities, and comfort—and the fitting out of the excellent marble bathrooms. The result is that you will enjoy a quiet night's repose with the aid of double glazing and ceiling fans in the most comfortable of attractively decorated rooms. Larger rooms can often accommodate an extra bed at a very reasonable price. A ground-floor room is wheelchair-friendly. The two suites, Kitty O'Shea and Charles Parnell, provide the most spacious accommodation in large rooms with ceilings so lofty that the bed occupies a mezzanine level above the bathroom. Breakfast is the only meal served but there is a "King family dining guide" for eating out. *Directions:* Harcourt Street leads from the southwestern corner of St. Stephen's Green and Harrington Hall is on your left. The hotel will fax driving directions. At the rear is a secure, off-road car park—let them know if you are arriving by car as parking is limited. See Dublin Walking Tour map for location.

HARRINGTON HALL
Owner: Henry King
70 Harcourt Street
Dublin, Ireland
Tel: (01) 475 3497, Fax: (01) 475 4544
28 Rooms, Double: €187–€290
Open: all year, Credit cards: all major
www.karenbrown.com/harringtonhall.html

For over 30 years Kilronan House has been offering visitors to Dublin a warm welcome. The Kinsella family are just the third owners of the place and they are constantly working to keep the house looking attractive and they strive very hard to keep up their reputation for cordial hospitality. Eight of the bedrooms are in the main house, all but two having snug en suite shower rooms—room 16 being a particularly attractive room with 2 queen beds. However, my choice would be to stay in one of the four rooms in the "new wing" that stretches behind the house. These have no view (in fact, instead of windows you have an expanse of glass-block walls) but they have a little more space and larger shower rooms. Naturally, there is a full Irish breakfast on the menu but the most popular items are pancakes with syrup and French toast. Gala recommends a variety of nearby restaurants that range from family restaurants and traditional pubs to special nights out on the town. A five-minute walk finds you at St. Stephen's Green, where you can stroll through the park to Grafton Street, the shopping heart of the town. *Directions:* From the east side of St. Stephen's Green go straight into Earlscourt Terrace and take the second right into Adelaide Road where you find Kilronan House on your right after 100 meters. Double-park in front to unload and you will be directed to the guesthouse's off-street parking. See Dublin Walking Tour map for location.

KILRONAN HOUSE
Owner: The Kinsella Family
70 Adelaide Road
Dublin, Ireland
Tel: (01) 475 5266, Fax: (01) 478 2841
12 Rooms, Double: €100–€170
Open: all year, Credit cards: all major
www.karenbrown.com/kilronan.html

Grand as life in Georgian Dublin may have been, it is surpassed at The Merrion, a dream of a hotel found in the heart of the city opposite Leinster House, home of Ireland's parliament. A few steps from bustling city streets and you are in vast drawing rooms enjoying traditional afternoon tea overlooking a tranquil expanse of garden and watching the gardener manicure the box hedges. If you are in the mood for the most sophisticated of meals, adjourn to the two-Michelin-star restaurant Patrick Guilbaud or enjoy more traditional Irish cuisine in The Cellar Restaurant after letting your hair down over a few drinks in The Cellar Bar. The Tethra Spa is an aptly named spot to assist guests in recovering from the revelry of the night before—swimming in the pool, working out in the gym, or enjoying a massage. It costs a small fortune to stay in one of the elegant suites in the "old building" while more affordable accommodation is found in the deluxe garden wing whose most attractive rooms open up to views of the loveliest of gardens. The hotel has the largest collection of Irish art outside the National Gallery. A traditional hotel in the heart of this vibrant city—what more could you ask from a place to stay? *Directions:* The Merrion is adjacent to Merrion Square, opposite Leinster House. Park in front of the hotel and the porter will take care of your car. See Dublin Walking Tour map for location.

THE MERRION
Manager: Peter MacCann
Upper Merrion Street
Dublin, Ireland
Tel: (01) 603 0600, Fax: (01) 603 0700
142 Rooms, Double: €410–€2450*
*Breakfast not included: €27
Dinner: €55
Open: all year, Credit cards: all major
www.karenbrown.com/merrion.html

Modern hotels are not usually included in this guide, but I was so taken with the value for money and excellent location offered by the Mespil Hotel that I decided to stay there, and I was very pleased with the quality of the accommodation and the friendliness of the staff. Sitting beside the Grand Canal with its grassy verges and leafy trees, the Mespil sports a pleasing modern exterior that complements its attractive contemporary interior. Dark-green leather sofas and stylish light-wood furniture deck the public rooms. The lunchtime carvery becomes the bar in the evening when the spacious restaurant offers a bistro-style menu. Bedrooms come in three varieties—front, back and side—and three colors—burgundy, green and gold. Front rooms face the canal (opt for one of these as it's a treat to have a view room in Dublin), while back and side rooms have slightly larger bathrooms. All standard rooms offer one double and one single bed. *Directions:* Follow signs for South City to Baggot Street. Cross the canal, turn right, and the Mespil is on your left after 200 meters. The hotel has a private car park and there is plenty of off-road parking available. See Dublin Walking Tour map for location.

MESPIL HOTEL
Manager: Martin Holohan
Mespil Road
Dublin, Ballsbridge, Ireland
Tel: (01) 488 4600, Fax: (01) 667 1244
255 Rooms, Double: €155*
*Breakfast not included: €12
Dinner: from €25
Closed: December 24 to 26, Credit cards: all major
www.karenbrown.com/mespil.html

A tall, creeper-covered wall and a discreet plaque are the only indications that you have arrived at 31 Leeson Close. Ring the buzzer, open the tall doors, and you enter an oasis of tranquility and greenery far from the clamor of the surrounding city. Number 31 was home to Ireland's famous 60s modern architect, Sam Stephenson, who fashioned it from two coach houses. Noel and Deirdre Comer, the present owners, have kept the cool, clean lines of this modern home. A contemporary painting hangs above the fireplace in the living room where the leather sofa, the only piece of furniture, hugs the wall of the conversation pit and stark, whitewashed brick walls contrast texturally with the mosaic tiled floor strewn with Oriental rugs. A great variety of bedrooms is spread over two buildings. The main house has grand, high-ceilinged rooms (I loved the spaciousness and decor of room 19 which faces the garden and 21 and 22 which face onto Fitzwilliam Street), while the coach house naturally has lower-ceilinged rooms, several of which have their own private patio. Noel, Deirdre, and Homer (the Labrador) work hard to give a gracious welcome and (Homer excluded) provide you with all the information you need on what to see and where to go in Dublin. *Directions:* Lower Leeson Street runs off the southern end of St. Stephen's Green. Leeson Close is opposite 41 Lower Leeson Street. A secure, off-road car park is adjacent to Number 31.

NUMBER 31
Owners: Deirdre & Noel Comer
31 Leeson Close
Dublin, Ireland
Tel: (01) 676 5011, Fax: (01) 676 2929
21 Rooms, Double: €190–€220
Open: all year, Credit cards: all major
Hidden Ireland
www.karenbrown.com/number31.html

Waterloo House is two tall Georgian townhomes cleverly combined to become a delightful guesthouse. Just a 15-minute walk to St. Stephen's Green and Trinity College, it is well set back from one of Dublin's quieter streets and has parking in front. Evelyn Corcoran and her friendly staff really look after their guests. Soft strains of classical music play in the lobby sitting room and there's an elevator for luggage and for those who do not want to climb as many as four flights of stairs. Whether your bedroom is on the garden level or at the top of the house, you'll be pleased with its smart décor. Rooms are cozy in size with king bedded rooms, overlooking the garden, being the most spacious. Breakfast is taken downstairs in the breakfast room that opens up to a sunny conservatory and gardens. Keycards give you access to the front door as well as your room so that you can come and go on your own timetable. There are lots of restaurants and bars within easy walking distance. *Directions:* Follow signs for South City. Cross the Baggot Street Bridge into Baggot Street. Pass a row of shops on your left and turn right into Waterloo Road—Waterloo House is on your left with a car park in front. See Dublin Walking Tour map for location.

WATERLOO HOUSE
Owner: Evelyn Corcoran
8–10 Waterloo Road
Dublin, Ballsbridge, Ireland
Tel: (01) 660 1888, Fax: (01) 667 1955
19 Rooms, Double: €114–€200
Open: all year, Credit cards: MC, VS
www.karenbrown.com/waterloo.html

Dating back to 1698, Grange Lodge is one of those large, comfortable houses that have evolved as owners have added and altered over the years. Today it's the home of Norah and Ralph Brown, easygoing, friendly folk who offer guests the warmest of welcomes. Norah has won many awards for her outstandingly good food and runs regular cooking classes. Be sure to book dinner when you make your reservations. Norah serves coffee in the lovely drawing room or in the den, a cozy room where, on colder evenings, a log fire bids a cheery welcome. The Browns are inveterate collectors and as a consequence lovely furniture, old china, pewter, stoneware, and fascinating bygones fill every nook and cranny. Upstairs are the very comfortable, individually decorated bedrooms, all with their own pretty bathrooms full of little extras. Acres of gardens ensure peace and quiet though it's just a minute's drive to main roads, making this an ideal touring base for the northern counties. Tour the nearby Tyrone crystal factory and try your own hand at cutting the hand-blown sparkling crystal. Nearby are two National Trust properties: Ardress House, a 17th-century manor, and The Argory, an 1820s house with a lot of original furniture. *Directions:* Take the M1 from Belfast to junction 15, take the A29 towards Armagh for 2 km, turn left at the Grange Lodge sign. Turn almost immediately right and Grange Lodge is the first white-walled entrance on the right.

GRANGE LODGE
Owners: Norah & Ralph Brown
7 Grange Road
Dungannon
Co Tyrone BT71 7EJ, Northern Ireland
Tel: (02887) 784212, Fax: (02887) 784313
5 Rooms, Double: £75–£79
Dinner: from £27 (not Sun)
Open: Feb to mid-Dec, Credit cards: MC, VS
www.karenbrown.com/grangelodge.html

Ann and Jim Mulligan built An Bohreen high on a hill with fabulous views. From the outside, it looks like a conventional bungalow; but once you are inside the dining room, you are presented with a wall of windows overlooking the bay of Dungarvan. The sitting room windows frame the Comeragh Mountains. Bedrooms are fresh and pretty with antique dressers and attractive bed linen. Jim is quintessentially Irish with a gleam in his eye, and a natural friendliness. He carries your bag, plans sightseeing, and answers questions; while Ann has a reputation for excellent cooking. A dinner here may well be the highlight of your trip. The four-course dinner must be reserved 24 hours in advance and is often wild salmon or Waterford lamb. Breakfasts are a real treat with warm scones and fresh-squeezed juice preceding the cooked dish with choices such as crepes with sautéed apples or the traditional "full Irish." Main roads will whisk you off to Waterford for sightseeing. You can stay close to home, visit local potteries, go hill walking or riding. Of course, you must see the local fairy bush covered with ribbons and bits that folks decorate it with. You drive your car down the hill, stop at the fairy bush, and your car starts to reverse up the hill on its own. Jim assures me it happens every time. *Directions:* From Waterford take the N25 towards Cork. Make a right turn 5 km from the "Resume Speed" sign as you leave the hamlet of Lemybrien.

AN BOHREEN
Owners: Ann & Jim Mulligan
Killeneen West
Dungarvan
Co Waterford, Ireland
Tel: (051) 291010, Fax: (051) 291011
4 Rooms, Double: €80–€85
Dinner: €38 (not Tue Jul to Aug)
Open: mid-Mar to Nov, Credit cards: MC, VS
www.karenbrown.com/anbohreen.html

You'll enjoy staying at Powersfield House on the outskirts of Dungarvan. Eunice has decorated her home with great style, she's a talented chef, and a warm, easy going person. When Eunice returned to Dungarvan to marry a local farmer they built this substantial neo-Georgian home large enough to provide plenty of space for their family on one side of the house and guests on the other. There are six most attractive bedrooms decorated with a modern flair in a traditional country house style. Downstairs guests have a comfortable sitting room adjacent to the dining room. Eunice is a talented chef who, until she had 3 young boys, ran a popular restaurant. Now she limits herself to dinner for guests though she is happy to give day-long cookery courses to parties of guests, demonstrating an arsenal of easy to prepare dishes for entertaining. Just down the road Dungarven is an attractive seaside town round a pretty bay. It's a particularly attractive coastal drive to Waterford and you can return by a faster, inland route. To the west is Ardmore, a 7th century monastic settlement. *Directions:* From Dungarvan take the Clonmel road. Powersfield House is the second turn to the left, and the first house on the right.

POWERSFIELD HOUSE
Owners: Eunice & Edmund Power
Ballinamuck
Dungarvan
Co Waterford, Ireland
Tel: (058) 45594, Fax: (058) 45550
6 Rooms, Double: €110–€120
Dinner: €27–€37
Open: all year, Credit cards: all major
www.karenbrown.com/powers.html

The summertime evening view from the dining room of Castle Murray House is simply staggering. As the night slowly draws in on green fields that tumble to the sea and scudding clouds dapple the reddening sky, the sun slowly sinks behind the distant Slieve League, the highest sea cliffs in Europe. The food is as outstanding as the view and served in portions that satisfy even the heartiest of Irish appetites. Owner Marguerite Howley's cooking attracts a large local following, so perhaps the best way to secure an often hard-to-come-by dinner reservation is to stay here. After an evening-long repast you can retire up the narrow pine staircase to one of the smartly decorated bedrooms with their sprightly contemporary decor and pleasing color schemes. Be sure to request a room with a view of the bay. If you want the most spacious of accommodation, opt for the "honeymoon room" found atop a narrow flight of stairs at the top of the house. While it does not have "the view" from its bedroom, it does from its spacious deck. Between breakfast and dinner the rugged Donegal landscape is yours to explore. *Directions:* From Donegal take the N56 towards Killybegs. The left-hand turn to Castle Murray House is in Dunkineely.

CASTLE MURRAY HOUSE
Owner: Marguerite Howley
Manager: Caroline Gullagher
Dunkineely, Co Donegal, Ireland
Tel: (074) 9737022, Fax: (074) 9737330
10 Rooms, Double: €120–€150
Dinner: €60 (not Mon or Tue in winter)
Closed: Christmas & mid-Jan to mid-Feb
Credit cards: MC, VS
www.karenbrown.com/castlemurray.html

Joe and Kay O'Flynn bought Rathsallagh House, a converted Queen Anne stables with 530 acres of farmland, in 1978. Encouraged by the spaciousness of the house, Kay opened three rooms for bed and breakfast guests and thus began a venture that has evolved into the country house hotel and golf club that you see today. Tractor sheds and barns are gone, replaced by a parade of bedrooms, and fields that lined the driveway are now the groomed fairways of the championship golf course. The billiard room, tennis court, Jacuzzi, sauna and capacious gardens encourage total relaxation. While the size of the operation makes it all seem rather grand, Rathsallagh manages to keep the bonhomie of a friendly, relaxed country house hotel complete with homey touches like Joe still paying his bills at the old pine table in the breakfast room. Begin the day with a lavish breakfast, choosing from an array of savory dishes on the sideboard. Relax with a drink before dinner and enjoy the comfortable country house style of the place. Realize that you deserve the best and stay in one of the deluxe stable rooms. It's just a 45 minute drive to the K Club where the Ryder Cup is being held in 2006. Sightseeing includes the Wicklow Mountains, Glendalough, and the National Stud. *Directions:* From Dublin airport take the M50 south the N7, which you exit for the M9 towards Carlow. After 9.5 km pass the Priory Inn on the left and just over 3 km later turn left for Rathsallagh.

❄ 🍵 ▦ ☎ P 🍴 ≋ 🏃 ⛳ ♿ 🎯 🏇

RATHSALLAGH HOUSE
Owner: The O'Flynn family
Dunlavin, Co Wicklow, Ireland
Tel: (045) 403112, Fax: (045) 403343
29 Rooms, Double: €270–€335
Dinner: €65
Open: all year, Credit cards: all major
www.karenbrown.com/rathsallagh.html

Monfin House is a real beauty of a Georgian home, restored with great care by Avril and Chris Stewart. It retains all the character of the elegant Georgian period, all the warmth of a family home and the luxury of super bedrooms. The two master bedrooms (Yellow and Peach) at the front of the house boast carved four-poster queen-sized beds, oodles of space and bathrooms with whirlpool tubs. Green and Blue are smaller, but only by comparison, with queen beds and especially large bathrooms with clawfoot tubs and separate showers. Sink into the sofas, set either side of the sitting room fire, and enjoy a drink. Avril enjoys cooking and whenever possible uses local and organic produce for breakfast. Enniscorthy is thriving town on the River Slaney dominated by Vinegar Hill from which there is a great view of the surrounding countryside. Winding streets lead to the Norman Castle home of the county museum. Nearby Wexford is famous for its operatic festival in October. There's no shortage of beaches to wander, gardens to visit or golf courses to play. *Directions:* From Enniscorthy take the N30 towards New Ross. After the big, grey disused granary take the next left up a hill. The entrance to Monfin House is on the right after 1 km.

MONFIN HOUSE
Owners: Avril & Chris Stewart
St John's
Enniscorthy
Co Wexford, Ireland
Tel: (054) 38982, Fax: (054) 38583
6 Rooms, Double: €130
Closed: Christmas, Credit cards: MC, VS
www.karenbrown.com/monfinhouse.html

Grim determination led me to Farran House—how could I get so lost?—but my endeavors paled into insignificance when I saw the amount of work it took, over a seven-year period, for Patricia and John to rescue this splendid Italianate house from ruin. They now live in a wing while guests can rent the main house on a self-catering basis or choose dinner, bed, and breakfast country house-style. Relax round the fire in the sitting room, enjoy a game of billiards in the former music room, and chat with fellow guests round the dining-room table. Upstairs, you find four lovely, spacious bedrooms all enjoying south-facing views across the valley. Room One is extra special because of its bathroom—a super-sized affair with a claw-foot tub sitting center stage. Your hosts have collected a picture library of all things Ireland—they travel the length and breadth of the country taking photos, which gives them an intimate knowledge of every scenic spot in the country—very handy for advising guests where to go and what to see. Blarney is 16 kilometers away, Kinsale and the coast about 40 kilometers. If renting an estate is not within range of your pocketbook, Patricia and John also have a three-bedroom cottage available. *Directions:* From Cork take the N22 towards Killarney for 15 km. Go around Ballincollig on the ring road and, after Dan Sheanhan's pub on your right, take the second right. Take the next right up the hill and the first gate is on your left.

FARRAN HOUSE
Owners: Patricia Wiese & John Kehely
Farran, Co Cork, Ireland
Tel: (021) 7331215, Fax: (021) 7331450
4 Rooms, Double: €140–€200
1 Cottage: €500–€690 weekly
Dinner: €40 (not Sun or Mon)
Open: Apr to Oct, Credit cards: all major
Hidden Ireland
www.karenbrown.com/farran.html

Catherine helped her mother in the antiques trade for many years and as her interest in furniture grew, so did her collection which is now large enough for her to theme her rooms depending on the period of the furniture: Art Nouveau, Victorian, Edwardian, Georgian and Regency. Having a fondness for Edwardian furniture I was particularly impressed by its spaciousness and the flat screen TV ideally placed for watching telly from the bed. A real prize is the Georgian room with its two beautiful commodes giving pride of place in this stately room with its V'Soske carpet and grand bathroom. If you want total peace and quiet opt for the garden suite, a large room decorated in vivid yellow and royal blue with a bay window large enough to accommodate two armchairs overlooking a sheltered corner of her vast garden. Catherine's style is ornate with grand gilded pieces and high-backed library chairs arranged before the fireplaces in each of the two sitting rooms. Her collecting is not limited to furniture, she has a whole array of silver and china which gives a great sense of occasion to breakfast in the dining room. Breakfast is the only meal served, which is no problem as there are several good restaurants close by. Guests often go the 6.5 kilometers into Galway city for city life and take day trips to the Aran Islands or to Connemara. *Directions:* From Galway take the N59 towards Clifden for 6.5 km and Killeen House is on your right.

KILLEEN HOUSE
Owner: Catherine Doyle
Bushypark
Galway, Ireland
Tel: (091) 524179, Fax: (091) 528065
6 Rooms, Double: €160–€190
Closed: Christmas, Credit cards: all major
www.karenbrown.com/killeen.html

Desmond, the 29th Knight of Glin's demesne is a 400-acre farm and late-18th-century castle stretching along the banks of the River Shannon. Staying here affords you the opportunity to live luxuriously—the house is an absolute beauty, full of exquisite furniture, family portraits, and beautiful artifacts. It is all very grand but not at all stuffy, for your host is Bob Duff, a gregarious New Zealander who ensures that you are well taken care of and well fed. He will give you a tour of the house with lots of suitably embellished stories. If you are passionate about art, literature, furniture, or books, be sure to ask if the Knight is in residence, for Desmond is happy to meet with guests when he is at home. Sip tea in the grand drawing room or curl up with a good book in the oh-so-comfortable sitting room. Bedrooms range from large and luxurious with extra-large bathrooms and dressing rooms to small and, by comparison, more ordinary. Ballybunion golf course is close at hand and the new Greg Norman-designed links course Doonbeg is an hour away via the Tarbert car ferry. *Directions:* From Limerick take the N69 towards Tralee for 50 km to Glin. At the end of the village turn left following the estate's wall to the castle entrance.

GLIN CASTLE
Owners: Olda & Desmond FitzGerald, Knight of Glin
Manager: Bob Duff
Glin, Co Limerick, Ireland
Tel: (068) 34173, Fax: (068) 34364
15 Rooms, Double: €280–€440
Dinner: €52
Closed: Nov to Mar, Credit cards: all major
Ireland Blue Book
www.karenbrown.com/glin.html

This dazzling, three-story Regency house, formerly the dower house of the Courtown estate, has an atmosphere of refined elegance created by vivacious hostess Mary Bowe and her delightful daughters Margaret and Laura. Mary has great charm and energy— during our stay she chatted with guests before dinner, made the rounds during dinner, and was back again at breakfast checking up to make certain that everything was perfect. The house is full of antiques, classic pieces that transport you back to the days of gracious living in grand houses. While we especially enjoyed our large, twin-bedded room with impressive, well-polished furniture, elegant decor, and a grand bathroom, I found the other bedrooms equally attractive. Six prized units are the ultra-luxurious, gorgeously decorated, extravagantly priced State Rooms tucked away in a separate ground-floor wing: request the Print Suite, Stopford, Georgian, or French. Dinner is served in the ornate Gothic conservatory dining room—all greenery and mirrors. The food is a delight—superb French and Irish dishes. An atmosphere of formal extravagance prevails. *Directions:* Marlfield House is 88 km from Dublin. Take the N11 south to Gorey. As you enter the town turn left, before going under the railway bridge, onto the Courtown Road, straight across the roundabout, and the house is on your right after 2 km.

MARLFIELD HOUSE
Owners: Mary, Ray, Margaret & Laura Bowe
Courtown Road
Gorey, Co Wexford, Ireland
Tel: (055) 21124, Fax: (055) 21572
20 Rooms, Double: €275–€765
Dinner: €62
Closed: mid-Dec to Feb 1, Credit cards: all major
Relais & Châteaux, Ireland Blue Book
www.karenbrown.com/marlfield.html

As newlyweds, Philomena and her husband John put in an exceedingly low bid on a very tumbledown Woodlands Farmhouse and it was many years before she found out why their offer had been accepted. To hear why and enjoy intriguing tales of gold sovereigns, cursed families, and arranged marriages, you will have to go and stay and ask Philomena for a story session with tea or coffee and scones upon arrival. What started out as a simple bed and breakfast has now grown into a very professional guesthouse. Guests have a cozily cluttered parlor with an eclectic assortment of sizeable Victorian chairs. The parlor opens up to an expansive dining room lit by two grand crystal chandeliers, which overlooks the lovely back garden. The front garden is even more impressive: a grand sweep of lawn with shrubs and trees going down to the river and the tennis court. All the smartly decorated bedrooms enjoy garden views and range in size from large family rooms to snug twins—all have electric blankets and small en suite shower or bathrooms with hairdryers. Room 6 is a particularly spacious room overlooking the back garden. In Wexford you can visit Wexford Heritage Park or Johnstown Castle Museum. To the north lies the Vale of Avoca where the television series Ballykissangel is filmed. *Directions:* Woodlands Country House is signposted on the N11 between Arklow (10 km) and Gorey (6 km). It is just before the village of Killinierin, 2 km west of the N11.

WOODLANDS COUNTRY HOUSE
Owner: Philomena O'Sullivan
Gorey, Killinierin, Co Wexford, Ireland
Tel: (0402) 37125, Fax: (0402) 37133
6 Rooms, Double: €100–€120
Open: Apr to Oct, Credit cards: MC, VS
www.karenbrown.com/woodlands.html

This is not your "Hollywood" of frantic freeways and homes of the rich and famous—this is the County Down version: a very nice town facing the sea backed by pastoral countryside. Here Beech Hill House, a Georgian-style dower house built for Victoria's grandmother, sits atop a little knoll. As we sat in the conservatory enjoying tea and fruitcake, I found it hard to believe that half an hour earlier I had been in the heart of Belfast. Victoria grew up just down the road on what is now the site of the Ulster Folk Museum so she is an expert on what to see and do in the area. She also has a real flair for decorating and her lovely home is filled with enviable family furniture. Bedrooms are on the ground floor and have all the right stuff: lovely furniture, books, hairdryers, TVs, goodies, firm beds (a zip-link twin/king, a double, and a queen), fine Irish linen, and well-proportioned bathrooms. We were up at dawn for a flight and Victoria insisted that we start our day with a "little" breakfast: the sideboard was groaning with bowls of fruit, yogurt, and fresh-baked bread accompanied by homemade jam...and then we moved on to the cooked items! For week long stays consider the Colonel's Lodge, a two-bedroom cottage in the garden. *Directions:* Leave Belfast on the A2 in the direction of Bangor. Bypass Holywood and about 2.5 km after going under the bridge at the Ulster Folk Museum turn right signed to Craigantlet. Beech Hill House is 3 km along on the left.

BEECH HILL HOUSE
Owner: Victoria Brann
23 Ballymoney Road, Craigantlet
Holywood BT23 4TG, Northern Ireland
Tel & Fax: (028) 9042 5892
3 Rooms, Double: £70–£80
1 Cottage: £300–£400 weekly
Open: all year, Credit cards: MC, VS
www.karenbrown.com/beechhill.html

The King Sitric is Ireland's premier fish restaurant, so here you can enjoy wonderful seafood then be lulled to sleep by the sea just 20 minutes from Dublin airport. Take an aperitif at the long tasting table in the wine cellar while perusing the menu, and then go upstairs to dine in the restaurant with its sweeping views over Dublin Bay. Aidan and Joan explain their food philosophy: "We have built up a network of suppliers of the finest Irish produce. Most of the fish is landed here at Howth. Our smoked salmon is smoked by McLoughlins on the West Pier and crab comes from John Sheridan who fishes Balscadden Bay a stone's throw from our door. Our Irish vegetables and meats are locally produced and mostly organic." After dinner enjoy a gentle stroll down the pier before retiring to bed in rooms named after Irish lighthouses. You'll find lots of polished wood and natural materials with subtle nautical touches. All bedrooms have sea views though Rockabill and Fasnet, the largest rooms at the top of the house, have the best. It's an excellent base for visiting Dublin—a 10-minute walk brings you to the Dart station for a 25-minute ride to Trinity College. Howth marina is just three minutes away by foot, while a more energetic hike takes you up the cliff path to Howth Head. *Directions:* From Dublin airport take the M1 towards Dublin and leave at the first exit, N32, for Malahide Road and Howth. At Howth haborfront you will find the King Sitric on your right.

KING SITRIC
Owners: Joan & Aidan MacManus
East Pier
Howth, Co Dublin, Ireland
Tel: (01) 832 5235, Fax: (01) 839 2442
8 Rooms, Double: €150–€210
Dinner: €55 (not Sun)
Open: all year, Credit cards: all major
Ireland Blue Book
www.karenbrown.com/kingsitric.html

Glenlohane is a lovely Georgian home of spacious but not overly grand rooms, sitting in beautiful, parklike grounds. It is a comfortable house, full of attractive things—lovely antiques and furniture, fires, and rooms in cheerful colors. Hosts Desmond and Melanie—the tenth generation of the family who built the house—are most welcoming, as are their dogs. Enjoy tea by the fire in the drawing room, play a tune on the grand piano, and immerse yourself in the charm of it all. Alternatively, browse through Melanie's herbs or sit in the tranquility of the walled garden. A family, or small group of friends, can reserve the entire house. Garden lovers are directed to Anne's Grove gardens at Castletownroche and Garinish Island with its grand Italianate gardens. Glenlohane is a working farm of 300 acres with cattle, sheep, horses, and hens; as well as barley, wheat, and oats. Outdoor activities include fishing, golf, horse shows, and agricultural shows. There is also a character cottage of three bedrooms and two bathrooms available for self-catering. It is handicap accessible and guide dogs are welcome. *Directions:* From Kanturk take the R576 toward Mallow. Very soon, bear left at the religious monument towards Buttevant on the R580. Take the first right at Sally's Cross towards Ballyclough. Glenlohane is the first residential entrance on the left after 2.5 km—the house does not have a sign.

GLENLOHANE
Owners: Melanie & Desmond Sharp Bolster
Kanturk, Co Cork, Ireland
Tel: (029) 50014, Fax: (029) 51100
4 Rooms, Double: €200
1 Cottage: €750 weekly
Open: all year, Credit cards: all major
Hidden Ireland
www.karenbrown.com/glenlohane.html

This delightful restaurant and bar with a number of cleverly designed guestrooms is found in one of the traditional buildings that front Kenmare's main street. Downstairs the restaurant serves a mixture of traditional (Irish stew, blackberry and apple pie) and Continental (seafood, pasta, tiramisu) food in a spiffy art-deco setting. Bedrooms are found upstairs at the back of the building, guaranteeing a quiet night's sleep. The rooms are ingeniously designed with all the mod cons. My preference is for the bedrooms on the top floor, their skylight windows providing lots of light and views of nearby rooftops and chimneys. Kenmare's interesting shops are on your doorstep and County Kerry is yours to explore. While you are in this area be sure to visit the Beara Peninsula and Garinish Island with its spectacular gardens. *Directions:* Kenmare is about a three-hour drive from Shannon on the N71 between Killarney and Bantry. From Bantry, Davitts is on your left as you drive through the town (Henry Street is one way). Parking is round the back.

DAVITTS
Owners: Mary & Donal Cremin
Henry Street
Kenmare, Co Kerry, Ireland
Tel: (064) 42741, Fax: (064) 42756
11 Rooms, Double: €80–€90
Dinner: €30
Closed: Dec 23 to 27, Credit cards: all major
www.karenbrown.com/davitts.html

The Irish name for Kenmare, An Neidin, means "the little nest" which is a good description of this attractive town nestling beside the River Kenmare at the foot of some of Ireland's most spectacular scenery. On the Cork road, out of the main bustle of town, The Lodge (purpose-built as a guesthouse and a substantial family home for the Quills and their four young sons) sits back from the road in 2 acres of grassy garden. Finbar works in the family's woollen shop in town, which has the largest selection of sweaters in Kenmare, if not all of Kerry, while Rosemary runs the bed and breakfast. She is exceedingly personable as is her staff of local ladies. Not a thing in the place (with the possible exception of two gigantic vases) is older than the house, from the traditional furniture to the portraits that line the staircase. Bedrooms are spacious and have large, top-of-the-line bathrooms. All have queen-size beds (one a grand four-poster) and nine are large enough to accommodate an additional single bed. One ground-floor bedroom is specially equipped for the handicapped. Kenmare is ideally placed for touring the Ring of Kerry and the prettier Beara Peninsula, as well as for visiting several historic houses and gardens including Muckross House and Derrynane House, home of Daniel O'Connell. *Directions:* Kenmare is about a three-hour drive from Shannon on the N71 between Killarney and Bantry. The Lodge is on the (Cork road) opposite the golf club.

❄ ☎ ✎ CREDIT ☎ P ⛷ ✝ 🎿 👫 🐎 ⚓

THE LODGE
Owners: Rosemary & Finbar Quill
Killowen Road
Kenmare, Co Kerry, Ireland
Tel: (064) 41512, Fax: (064) 42724
11 Rooms, Double: €90–€120
Open: Mar to Nov, Credit cards: MC, VS
www.karenbrown.com/lodge.html

The Park Hotel has come a long way since it began life in 1897 as the Great Southern Hotel Kenmare to provide a convenient overnight stop for railway travelers en route to or from the Ring of Kerry. Guests are greeted by a blazing coal fire, which casts its glow towards the cozy bar and lounge, and you sit down at a partners' desk to register before being shown to your room. Such touches give a small-hotel feeling to this larger establishment. Exquisite accommodations are provided in nine very luxurious suites with splendid views out over Kenmare Bay. Just as lovely are the superior bedrooms in the old house, many of which have bedrooms and an arch to the seating area—these also all have wonderful views of the bay. Rooms in the "newer" wing have balconies or patios to capture sideways bay views. The restaurant produces some of the finest food that you will find in Ireland. The Park provides programs for the Christmas and New Year holidays. Pamper yourself at the adjacent Sámas spa where you choose from over 40 holistic treatments. Use of the Thermal Suite (sauna, steam, aromatherapy mist and vitality pool with body, foot, and neck massage) is scheduled before your treatment and afterwards you relax on a day bed overlooking the woodlands. The spa has two couples private day suites. Beside the hotel is an 18-hole golf course. *Directions:* Kenmare is about a three-hour drive from Shannon on the N71 between Killarney and Bantry.

THE PARK HOTEL KENMARE
Owner: Francis Brennan
Manager: John Brennan
Kenmare, Co Kerry, Ireland
Tel: (064) 41200, Fax: (064) 41402
49 Rooms, Double: €480–€580
Dinner: €72
Open: Apr to Oct & Christmas, Credit cards: all major
Ireland Blue Book
www.karenbrown.com/parkhotel.html

Kenmare is one of my favorite Irish towns, and how appropriate that several of my favorite bed and breakfasts are located here, amongst them Sallyport House. Janie Arthur returned home after working for 15 years in California to help her brother, John, convert the family home into a luxurious bed and breakfast, decorating it in an uncluttered, sophisticated style. It's a family affair with John's wife Helen (who runs O'Sullivans pub at nearby Kilmakilogue) and sister Wanie and her children lending a hand. Return in the evening to chat round the fire in the drawing room or curl up in one of the comfortable chairs in the less formal sitting area with its exposed stone wall and old photographs of Kenmare. Breakfast is the only meal served—for dinner, it's a two-minute walk into town. The bedrooms are delightful, each furnished with antiques and accompanied by a large luxurious bathroom. Muxnaw has views of Muxnaw Mountain and deep window seats, Ring View looks out to the River Kenmare, Reen a Gross has an American king-sized four-poster bed, The Falls has a view of the pretty garden. It's delightful to stroll along the riverbank, through the park, and back through the town. You can spend several days exploring the Beara Peninsula, Ring of Kerry, and lakes of Killarney. *Directions:* From Killarney, follow Bantry signposts through Kenmare and Sallyport House is on your left before you come to the bridge.

SALLYPORT HOUSE
Owners: Janie & John Arthur
Kenmare, Co Kerry, Ireland
Tel: (064) 42066, Fax: (064) 42067
5 Rooms, Double: €140–€170
Open: Apr to Oct, Credit cards: none
www.karenbrown.com/sallyport.html

Sea Shore Farm, run by Mary and Owen O'Sullivan, is a particularly peaceful place to stay, no more than five minutes drive from Kenmare or a fifteen minute walk to town by a quiet side road. On arrival you are welcomed with a cup of tea or coffee "to settle you in" and given plenty of information on what to do in and around Kenmare. The lounge, overlooking the Kenmare Bay, has lots of literature on the area. The bedrooms look over the fields across the River Kenmare to the mountains of the Beara Peninsula where the roads are quieter and the scenery very similar to that on the Ring of Kerry. The two downstairs rooms have patios and are wheelchair compatible. It's a blissfully quiet and rural place to stay yet close to the bustle of Kenmare with its excellent restaurants, pubs, and shops. You are just off the Ring of Kerry. If you do not want to deal with coaches and lots of other traffic head for the Beara Peninsula where you get quieter roads and spectacular views. *Directions:* From Kenmare take the Killarney road (N71) for 300 meters. Pass the Esso petrol station on your right and take the next left onto the Ring of Kerry. Sea Shore Farm Guesthouse is signposted to your left after 300 meters.

SEA SHORE FARM GUESTHOUSE
Owners: Mary Patricia & Owen O'Sullivan
Kenmare, Tubrid, Co Kerry, Ireland
Tel & Fax: (064) 41270
6 Rooms, Double: €100–€130
Open: Mar to Nov, Credit cards: MC, VS
www.karenbrown.com/seashore.html

We continue to receive rave reviews on Shelburne Lodge praising not only the high quality of the decor, but also the delicious breakfasts. The building, a Georgian farmhouse, is lovely and the grounds with their lawns, herb garden, and tennis court are very attractive, but it is the interior that is outstanding. The polished wooden floors gleam and lovely antiques grace the sitting room and hallway. Admire Maura's enviable art collection—all by local artists. Each lovely bedroom is accompanied by a luxurious bathroom, each with a different color scheme. Of course, the towel rails are heated and you'll find books of just the sort you want to read and browse through in your room. The same attention to detail goes into the scrumptious breakfast she prepares—even the compote of fresh fruits is artfully garnished. Husband Tom is helpful and friendly, always there with a map and pointing guests in the right direction. Kenmare has some excellent restaurants and Maura as former chef at one of the best (Packies) is happy to make recommendations (advance reservations are a must). Maura also helps her sister Grainne at The Purple Heather, a great venue for lunch or snacks. After dinner wander into one of Kenmare's many pubs—there's entertainment and music to suit all tastes. *Directions:* Shelburne Lodge is on the R569 (Cork road) opposite the golf club.

SHELBURNE LODGE
Owners: Maura & Tom Foley
Kenmare, Co Kerry, Ireland
Tel: (064) 41013, Fax: (064) 42135
9 Rooms, Double: €130–€170
Open: Mar to mid-Dec, Credit cards: MC, VS
www.karenbrown.com/shelburnelodge.html

Behind a traditional downtown Kilkenny shopfront sits Zuni (the name of a native American tribe adopted on a whim by Paula), a swish complex of bar, restaurant, and accommodation where ornamentation is kept to a minimum. The narrow bar—the kind where you sip martinis rather than gargle pints of bitter—opens up to the restaurant, where vermilion-red walls contrast with black-and-cream decor and swathes of stainless steel can be seen in the adjacent kitchen. Of course, the food is modern and fun—more Mediterranean than Irish. You find the same modern, minimalist look in the bedrooms, all identically decorated in soft cream with a vermilion-red wall adding a splash of color behind the bed. Beds are heavenly, with crisp white cotton linens and plump duvets. Rooms are by and large snug in size so ask for 101 to 104 or 201 to 204, the larger rooms, or 300, the largest with a queen and two single beds and a big bathroom. Zuni's excellent central location allows you to walk to everything in town. *Directions:* Arriving in Kilkenny from Dublin on the N10, follow signs for City Centre, which bring you down John's Street. Cross the River Nore and you see the castle on your left. Go straight at the traffic lights into Patrick Street and Zuni is on your right after 200 meters. Park in front and collect a map that directs you to nearby parking.

ZUNI
Owners: Paula & Paul Byrne
26 Patrick Street
Kilkenny, Co Kilkenny, Ireland
Tel: (056) 7723999, Fax: (056) 7756400
13 Rooms, Double: €90–€170
Dinner: from €25
Closed: Christmas, Credit cards: all major
www.karenbrown.com/zuni.html

You would never dream that all the hurly-burly of Killarney town is just down the road when you look out of Coolclogher House to the rolling sheep pastures and distant hills of Killarney. Mary and Maurice Harnett hail from Ireland, and spent a good few years in London where Maurice restored homes in need of complete TLC, a skill he has honed to perfection with Coolclogher House—for the place was a complete disaster when they purchased it. Now it's in perfect condition with each spacious room stylishly decorated. I was especially enchanted by the dining room which opens up to a conservatory with a giant camellia that was a mass of pink blooms. While the Harnetts welcome individual guests on a bed and breakfast basis, do not be disappointed if you cannot secure a reservation for an individual room as they also rent the house on a self-catering basis (sleeps 10-12). When the house is rented the Harnett family decamps to a ground floor two-bedroom apartment. There's not a small room in the place which gives you lots of scope to make yourself comfortable. For dinner guests are directed to the great variety of restaurants in town. Whether viewed from a boat or a pony and trap, the lakes of Killarney are beautiful, but in summer the town can get very crowded. *Directions:* From Killarney take the Muckross road (N71) towards Kenmare. Take first left turn into Mill Road (after metal bridge). Gates on right after 1 km.

COOLCLOGHER HOUSE
Owner: Mary and Maurice Harnett
Mill Road
Killarney, Co Kerry, Ireland
Tel: (064) 35996, Fax: (064) 30933
5 Rooms, Double: €190–€240
1 House: €5,500 weekly
Hidden Ireland
www.karenbrown.com/coolclogher.html

Killarney is a pleasant town, best to explore after the crowds of daytime visitors have departed. Staying at Earls Court gives you the opportunity to go sightseeing out of town during the day, return in the evening for a cup of tea, and then walk into town for dinner. Emer and Ray built the house a few years ago and while the style outside is very modern, the inside is very traditional, for Emer is a great collector of lovely English and Irish antiques. Guests sign in at a writing desk once owned by President Cearbhaill O'Dalaigh. Many of the delightful bedrooms have balconies with views of the distant mountains across the trees. The larger, non-view rooms have the advantage of spacious sitting areas and bigger bathrooms. There's a fully equipped handicap room on the third floor. All bedrooms have lovely antique furniture, queen-sized beds (one is a four-poster and one an exquisite brass bed), excellent bathrooms with power showers, satellite TV, and phones. Several also have an extra single bed and two bedrooms have an interconnecting door, making them ideal for families. Golfers are spoiled for choice, with Killarney, Waterville, Dooks, Tralee, and Ballybunion the most popular courses, and there's a golf room for clubs. *Directions:* Arriving from Cork on the N22, take a left-hand turn 1 km before the first roundabout in Killarney (or go to the roundabout and retrace your steps). Proceed for 2 km and Earls Court is on your right.

EARLS COURT
Owners: Emer & Ray Moynihan
Woodlawn Junction
Killarney, Co Kerry, Ireland
Tel: (064) 34009, Fax: (064) 34366
18 Rooms, Double: €120–€190
Open: Mar to mid-Nov, Credit cards: MC, VS
www.karenbrown.com/earlscourt.html

You can be sure of being well fed when you stay at Ballymakeigh House for Margaret is a well know chef—she has written cookbooks, and operated a very successful local restaurant. Margaret uses only the finest local meats, fish and vegetables. She does a set four course dinner having discussed your likes and dislikes beforehand—there's an extensive wine list. At breakfast you'll be spoilt for choice. Relax in the sunny conservatory or on the Victorian sofas in the cozy sitting room, all decked out in shades of green. Bedrooms are named after local rivers and are all attractively decorated with well-chosen antique furniture, wallpaper, and fabrics—four have six-foot beds. There are masses of things to do in the area: Youghal (pronounced "yawl") is famous for its old buildings and Midleton Jamestown Centre tells the history of Irish whiskey production. You can motor up the coast to Waterford, down the coast to Kinsale and inland to Cashel and its famous rock. *Directions:* Killeagh is on the N25 between Youghal and Cork. Turn at The Old Thatch Tavern, then after 1 km turn right: Ballymakeigh House is on your right after 1 km.

BALLYMAKEIGH HOUSE
Owners: Margaret & Michael Browne
Killeagh, Co Cork, Ireland
Tel: (024) 95184, Fax: (024) 95370
6 Rooms, Double: €120–€130
Dinner: €45
Open: Feb to Nov, Credit cards: MC, VS
www.karenbrown.com/ballymakeighhouse.html

Flemingstown House, an 18th-century farmhouse, is just an hour's drive south of Limerick and Shannon airport, a quiet countryside world away from the hustle and bustle. Walk round the farm, watch the cows being milked, and chat with Imelda as she works in her spacious kitchen; for the two things that Imelda loves are cooking and taking care of her guests. It would be a shame to stay and not eat, for Imelda prepares tempting meals in which, following the starter and soup, there is a choice of meat or fish as a main course and always three or four desserts and farm cheeses made by her sister and her husband. The intricate stained-glass windows of the conservatory-style dining room were made by the same artist as those in the local church. Upstairs the bedrooms are top of the line, beautifully appointed and provided with a variety of twin and king-size combinations that can accommodate families of all sizes. Each bedroom has a small shower room. Nearby Kilmallock has the ruins of two friaries and the remains of its fortified wall weaving through the town. Guests find this a good base for touring counties Limerick, Tipperary, Kerry, and Cork. *Directions:* From Limerick take the N20 (Cork road) for 30 km and turn left to Kilmallock (10 km). From Kilmallock take the Kilfinane road (R512) for 3 km and the house is on your left.

FLEMINGSTOWN HOUSE
Owner: Imelda Sheedy-King
Kilmallock, Co Limerick, Ireland
Tel: (063) 98093, Fax: (063) 98546
5 Rooms, Double: €120–€140
Dinner: €45
Open: Feb to Nov, Credit cards: MC, VS
www.karenbrown.com/flemingstownhouse.html

Maeve Coakley purpose-built this fantastic bed and breakfast set high up over the town. In a place where accommodations are traditional, Maeve's is modern, bright and airy, decorated in utterly peaceful colors. The bedrooms were particularly alluring with their soft-white walls, linen curtains and bedcovers turned down to show Killarney wool blankets, crisp cotton sheets and large square pillows. The largest room is king-bedded with the rest being either queen or twin-bedded. All have immaculate bathrooms with power showers above the tubs, modem sockets, satellite TV, phone, a tea and coffee tray and a trouser press. There's a cozy little sitting room where you can chat by the fire. Breakfast has lots of good things on the menu: fresh fruits and juices, farmhouse cheese and yogurts, organic muesli and hot dishes with smoked salmon and scrambled eggs and catch of the day, as well as the traditional full Irish breakfast. There's several ways to walk into town where you can enjoy views across the sheltered harbor all manner of restaurants and a great many interesting shops. *Directions:* Go straight up the main street in Kinsale (Pearse Street) to the end, turn left and keep going till you see Fishy Fishy restaurant of the right and church on left. Follow the church wall to the left, narrow bend, and Blindgate House is on the left in 400m. There's lots of parking—a real bonus for Kinsale.

BLINDGATE HOUSE
Owner: Maeve Coakley
Blindgate
Kinsale, Co Cork, Ireland
Tel: (021) 477 7858, Fax: (021) 477 7868
11 Rooms, Double: €120–€170
Open: mid-Mar to mid-Dec, Credit cards: all major
www.karenbrown.com/blindgate.html

Sitting near the harbor, the Old Bank House occupies a prime heart-of-the-action location in this busy town. At one time these two Georgian townhouses served as a bank and the post office for the community, but now they have achieved a new lease of life as premier accommodation overlooking the sailboat-filled harbor. Here you are at the heart of town, having finally managed to secure a spot for your car on the street. On the ground floor guests have a little sitting area perfect for browsing through the menus from nearby restaurants and toasting their toes on a chilly evening. In the morning enjoy a lavish breakfast before heading out for the day. Bedrooms at the front enjoy the best views and the higher you go, the better the view over the roofs of the town—fortunately there is an elevator. The largest room is the Postmaster's Suite, with a spacious sitting area and fireplace. Beds are twin or king-sized if you request that the twin beds be zipped together. All the rooms have phone, TV, bath with shower over the tub, and Egyptian-cotton towels and bathrobes. The location at the very heart of this most attractive harbor town is ideal: you can stroll round the shops perusing the restaurant menus as you go. *Directions:* Follow the main road into Kinsale (Pearse Street)—the Old Bank House is on the right as you come into town. Parking is on the well-lit street.

OLD BANK HOUSE
Owner: Ciaran Fitzgerald
Pearse Street
Kinsale, Co Cork, Ireland
Tel: (021) 4774075, Fax: (021) 4774296
17 Rooms, Double: €170–€245
Closed: Christmas, Credit cards: all major
www.karenbrown.com/oldbankhouse.html

Beyond the yacht-filled harbor, the narrow streets of Kinsale terrace upwards to high ground. Here you find The Old Presbytery, the home of Noreen and Philip McEvoy who offer a choice of bed and breakfast or self-catering accommodation. The three-bedroom, three-bathroom self-catering apartments offer a sitting room with cheery gas fire in an antique grate, an extra bed that can be pulled down from a wall cupboard, and a kitchenette equipped with light cooking facilities. The Penthouse has a narrow circular staircase going from the living room to the bedrooms where you have views across the rooftops to the harbor (an excellent choice for a party of four). Bed and breakfast guests can choose accommodation that ranges in size from cozy to spacious (a family room with a double and two single beds), with all rooms found up a narrow staircase—leave your large cases in the car. Philip, who used to be a seafood chef, now concentrates his culinary efforts on breakfast, offering everything from traditional Irish fare to crepes filled with fruit in the breakfast room, where an antique Irish pine credenza takes pride of place. *Directions:* Go straight up the main street in Kinsale (Pearse Street) to the end, turn left, first right, and first right, and The Old Presbytery is on the right. Park in the yard.

THE OLD PRESBYTERY
Owners: Noreen & Philip McEvoy
43 Cork Street
Kinsale, Co Cork, Ireland
Tel: (021) 4772027, Fax: (021) 4772166
6 Rooms, Double: €100–€170
3 Apartments: €500–€1,000 weekly
Closed: Dec 1 to Feb 14, Credit cards: MC, VS
www.karenbrown.com/oldpresbytery.html

Laura and Andrew Corcoran have given a new lease of life to this grandiose Victorian edifice overlooking the harbor in Kinsale. Previous owners have all implemented their particular visions of grandeur and it is a tribute to the Corcorans' skills that they have consolidated all of the previous changes into a unified whole. A perky fire radiates a welcome in the vast reception hall (plenty of room for all guests to arrive at once) and the sitting and drawing rooms are large enough to provide a seating spot for every guest. Non-public rooms, however, are of more normal proportions. Bedrooms come in all shapes and sizes, from spacious junior suites to snug double rooms. All are attractively decorated in a traditional vein and priced according to their location—how wonderful if they all had harbor views! No matter—you step out the front door onto the harbor and into the heart of this lively town. Our favorite rooms are the four most luxurious tower suites—try to snag room 33 which has French doors opening to its own private courtyard. A buffet breakfast is included in the tariff and there is no shortage of restaurants nearby for dinner. *Directions:* Follow the main road into Kinsale (Long Quay)—Perryville House is on the right just as you come to the harbor. The hotel has several parking spaces opposite the hotel, next to the harbor.

PERRYVILLE HOUSE
Owners: Laura & Andrew Corcoran
Long Quay
Kinsale, Co Cork, Ireland
Tel: (021) 4772731, Fax: (021) 4772298
22 Rooms, Double: €200–€380
Open: Apr to Oct, Credit cards: MC, VS
www.karenbrown.com/perryville.html

On the next bay down the coast from the Cliffs of Moher sitting beside the bay is Moy House, a lovely hotel caressed by wispy breezes rising off the sea, with waves lapping at the bottom of the garden. Built as a stylish holiday home in the early 1800s, the property has undergone a complete transformation from one to two stories, with all but two bedrooms having superb sea views—several have window seats in the bedroom and the bathroom. Relax with a drink from the honesty bar in the chic drawing room and contemplate the delectable offerings on the menu before going down the narrow spiral staircase to the dining room. Downstairs bedrooms Kilmaheen and Kilfarboy are particularly spacious and have large bathrooms, with separate bathtubs and showers with dinner-plate-sized showerheads. Upstairs, Moymore is a favorite with lots of room and a window seat in its bay window. For the most spectacular view, clamber up the narrow stairs that take you to the top of the tower. At low tide wander along the quiet beach and round the headland to the bustling little holiday town of Lahinch. While golfers head for the popular Lahinch golf course, sightseers drive along the coast. Visit the Cliffs of Moher and The Burren. *Directions:* From Ennis take the N85 through Ennistymon to Lahinch. Go up the main street and take the first left, then turn left again following signposts for Miltown Malbay. After 2 km the entrance to Moy House is on the right.

MOY HOUSE
Manager: Bernie Merry
Lahinch, Co Clare, Ireland
Tel: (065) 7082800, Fax: (065) 7082500
9 Rooms, Double: €200–€290
Dinner: €48
Closed: Christmas to mid-Jan, Credit cards: all major
Ireland Blue Book
www.karenbrown.com/moy.html

Delphi Lodge with its surrounding estate was for centuries the sporting estate of the Marquis of Sligo. This wild, unspoilt, and beautiful valley with its towering mountains, tumbling rivers, and crystal-clear loughs was acquired in 1986 by Jane and Peter Mantle. Fortunately for those who have a love of wild, beautiful places, they have restored the Marquis' fishing lodge and opened their home to guests who come to walk, fish for salmon, relax, and enjoy the camaraderie of the house-party atmosphere. In the evening Peter often presides at the head of the very long dinner table (guests who catch a salmon take the place of honor) where guests enjoy a leisurely meal and lively conversation. A snug library and an attractive drawing room are at hand and guests often spend late-night hours in the billiard room. Bedrooms are all furnished in antique and contemporary pine. On a recent visit we especially admired rooms 3 and 4, two larger rooms with spacious bathrooms and fabulous views of the lake. Such is the popularity of the place that it is advisable to make reservations well in advance to secure a summer booking. Five deluxe, self-catering cottages are also available on the estate. *Directions:* Leenane is between Westport and Clifden on the N59. From Leenane go east towards Westport for 3 km, turn left, and continue along the north shore of Killary harbor towards Louisburgh for 8 km. Delphi Lodge is in the woods, on the left after the adventure center.

DELPHI LODGE
Owners: Jane & Peter Mantle
Leenane, Delphi, Co Galway, Ireland
Tel: (095) 42222, Fax: (095) 42296
12 Rooms, Double: €198–€258
5 Cottages: €550– €1,250 weekly
Dinner: €50
Open: mid-Jan to mid-Dec, Credit cards: MC, VS
Hidden Ireland
www.karenbrown.com/delphi.html

Rosleague Manor is a lovely Irish hotel—a comfortable country house hotel overlooking Ballinakill Bay and an ever-changing panorama of wild Connemara countryside. This is a quiet, sparsely populated land of steep hills, tranquil lakes, and grazing sheep, where narrow country lanes lead to little hamlets. Manager Mark Foyle is much in evidence, making certain that guests are well taken care of. The hotel is beautifully furnished with lovely old furniture, and the sitting rooms are cozy with their turf fires and comfortable chairs. The garden-style conservatory is a popular place for before- or after-dinner drinks. Bedrooms are most attractive, my preference being for those with views across the gardens to the sea and distant hills. The dining room is my favorite room in the house: tall windows frame the view and lovely old tables and chairs are arranged in groupings. There is an à-la-carte menu as well as the fixed-price menu that offers four or five choices for each course. Dishes vary with the seasons and include a wide selection of locally caught fish and Connemara lamb. This is a peaceful place to hide away and a well-located base for exploring the ruggedly beautiful countryside of Connemara. *Directions:* Take the N59 from Galway to Clifden then turn right at the church for the 10-km drive to Rosleague Manor.

ROSLEAGUE MANOR
Owner: Edmund Foyle
Manager: Mark Foyle
Letterfrack, Connemara, Co Galway, Ireland
Tel: (095) 41101, Fax: (095) 41168
20 Rooms, Double: €190–€250
Dinner: €45
Open: Easter to Nov, Credit cards: all major
Ireland Blue Book
www.karenbrown.com/rosleague.html

One of the joys of coming to stay with Beryl and James is that you get to see the completion of their various projects, first the house, then acres of gardens—the Japanese and French gardens, the conversion of the stables to a restaurant and the addition of seven suites opening in early 2007. The imposing house was built in the 1740s for the Cuffe family and was later the residence of the land agent who oversaw the Earl of Longford's estates. The upstairs drawing room boasts specially commissioned chandeliers and period furniture. Also on the first floor is a very spacious suite which has a sitting room with open fire and bathroom with antique bath. On the top floor Purple is the room to request not only for its vibrant color but also for its spaciousness. Breakfast is served at small tables in the ground-floor breakfast room with its beautiful fan-vaulted ceilings. Viewmount House is an ideal base for trips to Clonmacnoise, Birr Castle, and Newgrange. Garden enthusiasts head for Strokestown House with its 6 acres of gardens and Tullynally Castle with its Chinese and Tibetan Gardens. Longford's golf course is just across the back fence. *Directions:* Coming from the south, leave the N4 (Dublin to Sligo road) at the first roundabout in Longford towards Longford town. After the speed limit sign you see Viewmount House's sign. Turn very sharp left and the house is on your right in 500 meters.

VIEWMOUNT HOUSE
Owners: Beryl & James Kearney
Dublin Road
Longford, Co Longford, Ireland
Tel: (043) 41919, Fax: (043) 42906
13 Rooms, Double: €100–€160
Dinner: €55
Open: all year, Credit cards: all major
www.karenbrown.com/viewmount.html

Kilkenny is a most attractive, historic town, and there is no more perfect a base for exploring its many charms than Blanchville House, a 15-minute drive away. Acres of farmland give this handsome Georgian home seclusion. You'll know you've arrived when you see a tall, square, church tower-like folly. Inside Blanchville House, tall-ceilinged, generously proportioned rooms are the order of the day, and Monica is particularly proud of having several pieces of furniture that were made for the house. One of these is the glorious half-tester bed that graces the principal bedroom. Apparently Sir James Kearny, a great eccentric, was fond of waxing and singeing his mustache, an operation he performed in his bed. One day, while practicing this routine, he set fire to the bedding and narrowly escaped burning the house down. There's a portrait of Sir James in the drawing room, which has the lovely wallpaper hung in 1823: guests enjoy a drink here before going in to dine together round the long polished table. Three lovely self-catering cottages (one handicap friendly) are found in the old stables and gardener's cottage (sleeps 3 to 6). *Directions:* Leave Kilkenny on the N10 in the direction of Dublin and Blanchville House is signposted to your right after The Pike pub, 6 km out. Pass over the railway crossing, go 4 km and turn left at Connolly's pub, and the house is on your left after 2 km. There is no village of Maddoxtown and Dunbell is Connolly's pub.

BLANCHVILLE HOUSE
Owners: Monica & Tim Phelan
Maddoxtown, Dunbell, Co Kilkenny, Ireland
Tel: (056) 7727197, Fax: (056) 7727636
6 Rooms, Double: €100–€125
3 Cottages: €500–€700 weekly
Dinner: €40
Open: Mar to Nov, Credit cards: all major
Hidden Ireland
www.karenbrown.com/blanchville.html

The sheer size of Longueville House takes your breath away. Set on a hill overlooking the River Blackwater, this wonderful country house offers you the very best of Irish hospitality. It was built by Richard Longfield, who was spurred on to grander things by a sum of money he received for supporting the British Act of Union. The house is now owned by the O'Callaghan family whose forebears had the estate confiscated from them by Cromwell in 1650. The O'Callaghans take great pains to make sure that you enjoy your stay: Aisling makes certain you are well cared for and made to feel completely at home while William ensures that you are well fed. Longueville is almost completely self-sufficient with vegetables, salmon, lamb, and herbs coming from the estate. The dining room in soft shades of pink is a picture and extends into the Victorian conservatory (1862), while the adjacent library provides a snug place to dine. Each and every bedroom is beautifully decorated and accompanied by a splendid modern bathroom. Reservations can be made for salmon and trout fishing on the nearby Blackwater. There are several 18-hole golf courses within easy reach of Longueville. *Directions:* The hotel is located on the N72, 5 km west of Mallow on the Killarney road.

LONGUEVILLE HOUSE
Owners: Aisling & William O'Callaghan
Mallow, Co Cork, Ireland
Tel: (022) 47156, Fax: (022) 47459
20 Rooms, Double: €180–€360
Dinner: from €60
Closed: Jan 7 to Mar 15, Credit cards: all major
Ireland Blue Book
www.karenbrown.com/longuevillehouse.html

The 5-foot-thick wall in the dining room, the stone arch that leads to the kitchen, and the ancient defense wall in the garden are remnants of the 15th century keep that stood atop this rocky promontory. It's a "home" that has been added to over the years—a good bit of the house is over 300 years old with the most recent addition being shower rooms for each guest room. Beds are large and rooms are most attractively decked out. My favorite bedrooms were Lady Mary's room with its big bay window looking across the garden wall to miles of countryside and Deedee Walsh, a spacious room at the back. Joan and her daughter Catherine are the most welcoming and attentive of hostesses. They strongly believe in keeping you well fed: breakfasts have to be seen to be believed—a vast array of fruit dishes alongside fresh scones and a variety of hot dishes. Scones and a pot of tea (sometimes homemade pie) are served in the afternoon to keep you going between lunch and dinner. It's a delightful spot just a few minutes from the main roads that whisk you into Waterford and Cork. There are some lovely drives in this area (The Vee and Nire Valley to Clonmel) and several castles (Cahir and Lismore), and the sea with Dungarvan and Youghal is just over the hills. *Directions:* From Dungarven take the N72 towards Cork for 9.5 km (after Cappagh) and turn right on the R761 signposted Clonmel. After 5 km turn right in Millstreet, cross the bridge and the property is on your right.

CASTLE COUNTRY HOUSE
Owners: Joan & Emmett Nugent
Millstreet, Cappagh, Co Waterford, Ireland
Tel: (058) 68049, Fax: (058) 68099
5 Rooms, Double: €90–€100
Dinner: €30
Open: Mar to Nov, Credit cards: MC, VS
www.karenbrown.com/castlefarm.html

Amongst the scattered modern holiday cottages surrounding the village of Miltown Malbay, a popular Irish holiday destination; you find a traditional Irish farmhouse that is now a welcoming guesthouse, restaurant, and cookery school operated by Rita Meade. Rita offers cookery courses for adults, teenagers, and children. The heart of the house is the country kitchen with its large central island designed for cooking classes. There are comfortable chairs in the sitting room with its old country dresser. The adjacent dining room has been extended with a sunny conservatory. Dinner has four to five choices in each of the three courses. The country theme is continued in the bedrooms with their pine furniture and old beds topped with quilts. All bedrooms have televisions and compact shower rooms and three rooms have a double and a single bed. There is a small ground-floor double-bedded room for those who have difficulty with stairs. The nearby Cliffs of Moher are a great attraction but you can use Berry Lodge as a base for visiting Bunratty Folk Park, Craggaunowen Megalithic Centre, the Aran Islands, exploring The Burren, and sailing to Scattery Island. *Directions:* From Ennis (on the Limerick to Galway road) take the N85 to Inagh then the R460 to Miltown Malbay (32 km total). Take the N67 Spanish Point Road in the center of the village, pass the caravan park, cross the bridge, take the second left, and Berry Lodge is first on the right.

BERRY LODGE
Owner: Rita Meade
Miltown Malbay, Annagh, Co Clare, Ireland
Tel: (065) 7087022, Fax: (065) 7087011
5 Rooms, Double: €84–€88
Dinner: €40
Closed: mid-Jan to mid-Feb, Credit cards: MC, VS
www.karenbrown.com/berry.html

Lough Owel Lodge is a modern house set between Lough Owel and a quiet country road that runs into Mullingar. While the house has no architectural distinction, this is a tranquil country spot where you can cycle down quiet roads, stroll the shores of Lough Owel, and generally enjoy the peace and quiet of the center of Ireland. Aideen and Martin Ginnell find that the house works really well for raising a family of four children and providing bed and breakfast; for it is divided into two parts, the front being for guests and the back for their family. I particularly appreciated the large car port which sheltered me from the rain as I arrived. A large sitting room with comfortable sofas and floor-to-ceiling windows offering views of the garden and lake adjoins the dining room with its lovely old table and chairs. Upstairs, the two premier rooms are Lough Ennell with its king-sized, four-poster bed and Lough Owel with its family heirloom mahogany half-tester double bed. A family suite consists of a small double bedroom leading to a small twin-bedded room and a bathroom. Guests often wander down to the lough, enjoy a game of tennis, and make use of the children's game room. Tullynally Castle, Carrickglass Manor, Belvedere House, Fore Abbey, and Athlone Castle are within an hour's drive. *Directions:* Take the N4 from Dublin towards Sligo. After passing the third exit for Mullingar, Lough Owel Lodge is signed to your left after 1 km.

LOUGH OWEL LODGE
Owners: Aideen & Martin Ginnell
Mullingar, Cullion, Co Westmeath, Ireland
Tel: (044) 48714, Fax: (044) 48771
5 Rooms, Double: €70–€76
Open: Apr to Oct, Credit cards: MC, VS
www.karenbrown.com/loughowel.html

Readers' letters praise the warmth of welcome, the delectable food, the quality and utter charm of this country house—and the fact that Mornington is an hour and a half's drive from Dublin airport, making it an ideal first or last destination in Ireland. I totally concur; for a stay at Mornington House with Anne and Warwick, the fifth generation of his family to call this home, is also something I find completely delightful. The O'Haras have an easy way of making guests feel at home. They chat with them in the drawing room after dinner, and put a lot of trouble into helping them with their activities and sightseeing in this unspoiled region with its lakes, canals, and gently undulating countryside. Anne is a talented cook, producing delicious dinners and outstanding breakfasts. Families are welcome and children can be served an early tea. The two front bedrooms are enormous: one has a large brass bed sitting center stage which requires a climb to get into it, while the other has a Victorian double bed and shares the view across the peaceful grounds. The third bedroom, a delightful twin-bedded room, looks out to the side garden and the woods. The oldest wing of the house contains two smaller bedrooms overlooking the kitchen garden. *Directions:* From Dublin take the Sligo Road to the Mullingar bypass. Exit for Castlepollard and go 10 km to Crookedwood, where you turn left by The Wood pub. After 2 km turn right and Mornington is on your right after 1 km.

MORNINGTON HOUSE
Owners: Anne & Warwick O'Hara
Mullingar, Mornington–Multyfarnham
Co Westmeath, Ireland
Tel: (044) 72191, Fax: (044) 72338
5 Rooms, Double: €130–€150
Dinner: €42.50
Open: Apr to Oct, Credit cards: all major
Hidden Ireland
www.karenbrown.com/morningtonhouse.html

The O'Donnell family's picturesque farmhouse has great appeal. It is over 200 years old and has received a sensitive restoration. There's a snug little lounge with a low thick stone arch that was one of the original doors in the house attesting to the fact that folks must have been much smaller in days gone by. A bay window nook overlooks the front garden and provides a perfect place for laying out your map and planning the days activities, returning home for one of Ber's excellent home-cooked dinners. Upstairs there are three guest bedrooms: 1: a tiny double with en suite shower (usually rented as a single), 2: a snug twin with bathroom, and 3: a larger room with zip-link beds with an en suite shower room. Take a stroll round the lovely garden and walk down to and along the riverbank. Trout fishing is a great draw. Walkers head for the hills—Kilmaneen is surrounded by the Comeraghs, Knockmealdowns, and Galtee Mountains. Kevin can either take you out for the day in a group walking or supply you with maps. Sightseers have lots to keep them busy with driving The Vee and visiting Lismore, Cahir, Cappoquin, and Swiss Cottage. If you have a family, enquire about renting the adjacent little two-bedroom cottage, either for bed and breakfast or on a self-catering basis. *Directions:* Go through Newcastle, towards Cloheen, at the Y-junction bear right down a narrow, winding lane, and Kilmaneen is on your right after 2 km.

KILMANEEN FARMHOUSE
Owners: Bernadette & Kevin O'Donnell
Newcastle, Clonmel, Co Tipperary, Ireland
Tel & Fax: (052) 36231
3 Rooms, Double: €85
1 Cottage: €525 weekly
Dinner: €25 not Sun
Open: Apr to Dec, Credit cards: MC, VS
www.karenbrown.com/kilmaneen.html

When Lord Inchiquin sold Dromoland Castle in 1963, he moved five minutes up the hill to Thomond House, a large Georgian-style mansion. Now it is home to his nephew Conor O'Brien (the present Lord Inchiquin and head of the O'Brien chieftancy) and his family—and what a delightful home it is, with its high-ceilinged rooms looking out through tall windows to the surrounding countryside. An air of quiet formality is the order of the day. Guests enjoy a comfortable drawing room, take breakfast in the dining room, and watch television in the library. A sweeping staircase leads to the upper gallery and bedrooms, which are beautifully outfitted and offer views of the parkland or the adjacent castle. Two additional lovely bedrooms are found on the ground floor. You might want to walk down to Dromoland Castle for a superbly formal meal or drive a few kilometers further to less expensive restaurants. Guests often play golf on the neighboring course or roam over the estate, while farther afield lie the dramatic Cliffs of Moher, The Burren, Lahinch, Doonbeg and Ballybunion golf courses. *Directions:* The Dromoland Estate is just off the N18, Ennis to Limerick road, 13 km north of Shannon airport. The entrance to Thomond House is south of Dromoland Castle.

THOMOND HOUSE
Owners: Helen & Conor Inchiquin
Newmarket-on-Fergus, Co Clare, Ireland
Tel: (061) 368304, Fax: (061) 368285
5 Rooms, Double: €240–€380
Dinner: €80
Closed: Christmas, Credit cards: all major
www.karenbrown.com/thomondhouse.html

Built on a sheltered site with distant views across Strangford Lough to the Mourne Mountains, Edenvale House is the lovely home of a most gregarious couple, Diane and Gordon Whyte. Relax with tea and cakes in the beautiful drawing room, plan your sightseeing forays, and enjoy the complete tranquility of this lovely spot. Try to snag one of the spacious front bedrooms with their spectacular views, dressing rooms large enough to accommodate a bed for a child, and spacious bathrooms with both bath and shower. (One's a queen-size four-poster, the other a king or twin.) The two other very lovely bedrooms have garden views and spacious shower rooms. There's a beautiful garden to wander in and horses and ponies to enjoy. Just down the road, Mount Stewart House has a splendid interior and a painting by Stubbs, but the acres of magnificent gardens are the main attraction. Nearby, the village of Greyabbey has lots of antique shops and the ruins of a Cistercian abbey. Dozens of old buildings have been brought from the countryside to the Ulster Folk Park where demonstrations of traditional crafts and farming are given. *Directions:* From Belfast take the A20 through Newtownards in the direction of Portaferry. After 3.2 km the entrance to Edenvale House is on the left.

EDENVALE HOUSE
Owners: Diane & Gordon Whyte
130 Portaferry Road
Newtownards
Co Down BT22 2AH, Northern Ireland
Tel: (028) 9181 4881, Fax: (028) 9182 6192
4 Rooms, Double: £70–£80
Closed: Christmas, Credit cards: MC, VS
www.karenbrown.com/edenvale.html

Eoin's great-great-grandfather came to the Nire Valley to build the church. He married a local girl Hanora and together they lived in a little cottage adjacent to the church nestled beside the tumbling River Nire in this delightfully wild and isolated spot on the edge of the Comeragh Mountains. They would not recognize their little home for it has been extended to include a parade of sitting rooms, spacious restaurant, hot tub for eight in the conservatory, and array of large bedrooms. All bedrooms have Jacuzzi bathtubs—just for fun, reserve one of the six rooms whose bathrooms come equipped with Jacuzzi tubs for two. Whenever you come to stay, you can be sure of being well fed—Mary, Eoin's mum, lays out a feast of a breakfast for which there is always a variety of freshly baked breads. In the evening Eoin (pronounced Owen) and his wife Judith offer a set, four-course, dinner with lots of choices for starters and main courses. Packed lunches, maps, and directions are available for walks that range from leisurely rambles to challenging hill hikes. Non-walkers can drive to Lismore, Cashel, or over The Vee, returning in time for a visit to one of the nearby pubs for a drink and perhaps (more often in the summer months) a late-night Irish music session. *Directions:* From Clonmel or Dungarvan, follow the R672 as far as Ballymacarbry, where you turn left at Melody's Lounge Bar. Travel 5.6 km and Hanora's is beside the church just before the stone bridge.

HANORA'S COTTAGE GUESTHOUSE
Owners: Mary, Judith & Eoin Wall
Nire Valley, Clonmel
Co Waterford, Ireland
Tel: (052) 36134, Fax: (052) 36540
10 Rooms, Double: €160–€250
Dinner: €47
Closed: Christmas, Credit cards: MC, VS
www.karenbrown.com/hanoras.html

Guests at Currarevagh House (pronounced "Curra-reeva") find themselves entering a world reminiscent of the turn of the last century. Tranquility reigns supreme and things are done the good old-fashioned way at Currarevagh House. However, do not be afraid that you will be deprived of central heating and private bathrooms, for this is not the case. If you book well in advance, you may be able to secure one of our four favorite rooms (1, 2, or 3 in the main house, or room 16 in the "new" wing with its lake views). There are several smaller rooms in the new wing. Try to arrive by 4:30 pm when tea and cakes are served—you will then have enough time for a brisk walk to make room for a delicious dinner at 8. A gong announces dinner and while there are no choices, the helpings are of generous proportions. A tempting breakfast buffet of cold meats, cheeses, and traditional cooked breakfast dishes is spread on the sideboard and the hotel is happy to pack you a picnic lunch for your day's excursion. It's all very old-fashioned and un-decorator-perfect, but I thoroughly enjoy it. Harry can arrange for fishing on the adjacent Lough Corrib, the second largest lake in Ireland, a haven for fishermen. *Directions:* From Galway take the N59 to Oughterard, turn right in the center of the village, and follow the lake shore for the 6-km drive to the house.

CURRAREVAGH HOUSE
Owners: June & Harry Hodgson
Oughterard, Connemara, Co Galway, Ireland
Tel: (091) 552312, Fax: (091) 552731
15 Rooms, Double: €190–€208
Dinner: €45
Open: Apr to mid-Oct, Credit cards: MC, VS
Ireland Blue Book
www.karenbrown.com/currarevaghhouse.html

Carmel is the sixth generation of her family to live in the Oughterard area and the first to be more interested in interior design than the Connemara ponies that her family has always raised. Named Railway Lodge because it stands adjacent to a former Railway line—now a walking path—the house has a modern exterior and country style interior. There's a snug parlor with a fire for inclement weather and a sunny conservatory overlooking the rolling gorse and distant mountains. Stylish bedrooms have queen-sized beds with crisp white sheets and duvets, and antique pine furniture—each with a top-of-the-line shower room. For dinner we walked the ten minutes into Oughterard and Carmel lent us a flashlight to guide us home. Breakfast proved to be a sumptuous affair. The offer of fresh-baked scones and bread and poached fruit led us to decline the offer of a cooked breakfast. If you have an interest in walking, local history or Connemara ponies, Carmel refers you to her father who lives just down the road. Lough Corrib is a popular fishing venue. Non-fisher types can enjoy spectacular drives through the rugged Galway countryside and sightseeing trips to islands on the lough. *Directions:* Arriving in Oughterard from Galway city you see the Corrib Hotel on your left, turn left immediately after and then immediate right (do not go straight). Continue to fork in road and take a right and Railway Lodge is the 2nd entrance on the left.

RAILWAY LODGE
Owners: Carmel Geoghegan & Joe Howlett
Canrower
Oughterard, Co Galway, Ireland
Tel: (091) 552945, Fax: none
4 Rooms, Double: €100–€110
1 Cottage: €540–€590 weekly
Open: all year, Credit cards: MC, VS
www.karenbrown.com/railway.html

Portlaoise has been bypassed with a new road and you can once again enjoy the quiet in this heart-of-Ireland town. Situated close to downtown on a side street, Ivyleigh House is set back from the road, its immaculate Georgian façade heralds a first-class interior furnished and decorated in a delightful traditional style. A lovely sitting room is available for guests' use and for breakfast there's a handsome dining room, its large communal table decked out with china and crystal. Dinah does an excellent breakfast with the freshest of local ingredients including free-range eggs, local bacon, and natural yogurt with geranium jelly. Then there's perfect porridge with cream, homemade brown bread, tea made with leaf tea, and freshly brewed coffee. The spacious bedrooms are particularly comfortable with top-of-the-line beds, linen sheets and pillowcases, and large shower rooms with power showers. One is located downstairs on the garden level. There is no shortage of restaurants for dinner. Portlaoise is well placed for visiting Telomere, Kildare, Kilkenny, and Carlow, the Slieve Bloom Mountains, Emo Court, and the Rock of Dunamase, an ancient fort. A 2 bedroom cottage at Killenard is available for weekly rental. *Directions:* Approaching from Cork, turn off the N8 for Portlaoise. In Portlaoise drive straight through two roundabouts onto the N80 for 30 meters, turn right at the railway bridge, and Ivyleigh House is the second house on the left.

IVYLEIGH HOUSE
Owners: Dinah & Jerry Campion
Bank Place, Church Street
Portlaoise, Co Laois, Ireland
Tel: (0502) 22081, Fax: (0502) 63343
6 Rooms, Double: €125
1 Cottage: €700–€750 weekly
Closed: Dec 23 to Jan 2, Credit cards: MC, VS
www.karenbrown.com/ivyleigh.html

On John's retirement, the Deanes demolished the holiday cottage they owned on this site and in its place built Croaghross, a stylishly modern building that captures the stunning views of Ballymastocker Strand, one of Donegal's loveliest beaches. While the house is of modern design, the interior is very traditional and furnished with antiques. In the evenings, an open fire burns in the large comfortable parlor where guests can relax. Two bedrooms capture the view (a double, a twin-bedded, and a family room) and each has French windows opening up to private patios. Another very spacious twin-bedded room is specially equipped for wheelchair access. For longer stays there is a three-bedroom cottage and a luxurious three-bedroom house. Guests often play golf on Portsalon golf course, which runs beside the beach. Enjoy spectacular ocean views as you drive round the Fanad Peninsula or traveling farther afield. *Directions:* From the outskirts of Letterkenny turn right for Ramelton and Rathmullen. Cross the bridge in Ramelton and turn left for Portsalon (25 km from Letterkenny). At the crossroads in Portsalon take the Fanad road for 1 km and just before the golf club turn left up a lane to Croaghross.

CROAGHROSS
Owners: Kay & John Deane
Portsalon, Co Donegal, Ireland
Tel & Fax: (074) 91 59548
5 Rooms, Double: €70–€100
2 Cottages: €500–€875 weekly
Open: mid-Mar to Oct, Credit cards: MC, VS
www.karenbrown.com/croaghross.html

Ardeen country house is situated in the heritage town of Ramelton overlooking the River Lennon. This Victorian house gives you a homey relaxed feeling the moment you walk through the front door. Ardeen is the onetime home of Nurse Black who was the private nurse to King George V. The book King's Nurse, Beggar's Nurse tells her story. Anne and Bert Campbell have been welcoming guests into their lovely home for many years. Anne enjoys baking and will spoil you with afternoon tea and home made scones as soon as you arrive. Breakfast is served around the beautiful antique dining table and includes fresh fruits, home made brown bread and scones as well as the traditional Irish breakfast. The bedrooms are all very nicely furnished and individually decorated and in keeping with the house. Four are en suite and a twin room enjoys a large private bathroom. The adjacent stable has been converted to a snug holiday cottage with an exposed stone living room, attractive kitchen and three bedrooms, one of which is en suite. Ardeen is an ideal base for exploring the Donegal coastline and visiting Glenveagh National Park and the Glebe Art Gallery with its fine collection of Irish paintings. *Directions:* If you are arriving from Donegal, take the N56 to Letterkenny and on the outskirts of the town look for the T72, signposted for Rathmullen. It's an 11-km drive to Ramelton. When you reach the river turn right, following the bank, and Ardeen is on your right.

ARDEEN
Owners: Anne & Bert Campbell
Ramelton, Co Donegal, Ireland
Tel & Fax: (074) 91 51243
5 Rooms, Double: €70–€80
1 Cottage: €350–€500 weekly
Open: Easter to Oct, Credit cards: MC, VS
www.karenbrown.com/ardeen.html

Frewin was a rectory for over 150 years and its earlier fortified annex dates back to the 1600s. Thomas, a restorer of old homes, antique collector, and raiser of rare-breed animals, found a family link while he was refurbishing the house: his great-aunt Susan had written her name on the back of one of the cupboards in the maid's room in 1912. If you do not mind having your own private shower room down the hall, you can stay in Aunt Susan's room. The other three bedrooms are small suites with sitting room areas— one has a claw-foot tub in the bathroom and the other two have showers. Our favorite, the green room, has a king-sized bedroom and, through the shower room, a private library which can double as a sitting room. There's lots of interesting furniture (a praying wall and sideboard from Glenveagh Castle) and pictures (the library is covered with old Vanity Fair prints). Regina and Thomas are hospitable and easygoing. Several of Thomas's finds are for sale in a little courtyard store. If you want to stay for a week, there are two little cottages tucked into quiet corners of the 2-acre garden. Ramelton is a 17th-century town with handsome houses and old riverside warehouses. A scenic route winds up Fanad Peninsula to Rathmullan and Portsalon. *Directions:* From Letterkenny take R245 towards Ramelton. Travel 11 km, pass the Shell station (on right), continue 800 meters and turn right at speed limit sign—Frewin is 400 meters along on the right.

FREWIN
Owners: Regina & Thomas Coyle
Ramelton, Co Donegal, Ireland
Tel & Fax: (074) 9151246
4 Rooms, Double: €120–€180
1 Cottage: €500–€550 weekly
Dinner: €45
Closed: Christmas, Credit cards: MC, VS
Hidden Ireland
www.karenbrown.com/frewin.html

Rathmullan House has a perfect setting amidst acres of gardens that slope down to a sandy beach, with views of the mountains across Lough Swilly. William and Mark are the second generation of their family to run it as a country house hotel. They have lots of youthful vitality and along with their wives, Yvonne and Mary, add a warm family presence. It's a delightfully rambling house with large sitting rooms (one in an Indian Raj style) leading to Batt's bar presided over by the portrait of Mrs. Batt who had Rathmullan house built as her summer home in the 1800s. Here you can enjoy drinks and lighter fare. Three-or four-course dinners are served in the dining room where meters of fabric are gathered into peaks dotted with soft lights to create the most romantic of dining atmospheres. Bedrooms are either "view" (garden and lough) or "not" and fall into three categories: Regency; (delectable, subtly themed, oh-so-spacious rooms with terrace or balcony and grand bathrooms of which the two penthouses offer the ultimate in luxury); Balcony (spacious rooms with top of the line bathrooms, terrace or balcony); or Main House (mainly high-ceilinged rooms divided between no view and lough view rooms—try to snag one with a spacious bay-window). Walk on the beach, swim in the pool, play tennis or enjoy a massage. *Directions:* From Letterkenny take the R245 through Ramelton and Rathmullan. The hotel is on the right as you leave the village.

RATHMULLAN HOUSE
Owners: Mark, Mary, William & Yvonne Wheeler
Rathmullan, Letterkenny
Co Donegal, Ireland
Tel: (074) 9158188, Fax: (074) 9158200
32 Rooms, Double: €170–€280*
Service: 10%
Dinner: from €42.50
Open: all year, Credit cards: all major
Ireland Blue Book
www.karenbrown.com/rathmullan.html

Hunter's Hotel has adopted Samuel Johnson's words as a creed and they certainly describe it: "There is nothing which has yet been contrived by man by which so much happiness is produced as by a good inn." Dating back to the 1720s, the hotel retains its old-world charm with creaking wooden floorboards, polished tile floors, old prints, beams, ancient sofas covered in old-fashioned chintz, and antique furniture. The Gelletlie family has owned the inn since 1820, and now Tom and Richard Gelletlie (the fifth generation) ably assist their mother, Maureen. There is a delightful feeling of another age, which endures in the tradition of vast, Sunday roast lunches (1 pm prompt: book ahead) and afternoon teas of oven-fresh scones and strawberry jam—a particularly delightful feast when enjoyed in the garden on a warm summer's afternoon. You can sleep in bedrooms that kings have slept in—the king of Sweden has paid several visits. I loved my room 17 a spacious ground floor twin. Be sure to request a room with a view of the flower-filled gardens stretching beside the hotel down to the River Vartry. Some interesting gardens and houses are a short drive away: Powerscourt with its grand gardens, Mount Usher with its informal gardens, and Avondale House with its wooded parklands. *Directions:* Take the N11 from Dublin to Rathnew and turn left in the village for the 1-km drive to Hunters Hotel.

HUNTER'S HOTEL
Owner: The Gelletlie family
Rathnew, Co Wicklow, Ireland
Tel: (0404) 40106, Fax: (0404) 40338
16 Rooms, Double: €190–€210
Dinner: €45
Closed: Christmas, Credit cards: all major
Ireland Blue Book
www.karenbrown.com/hunters.html

Tinakilly House maintains the purpose for which it was designed—gracious living. The house was built in the 1870s by Captain Robert Halpin, the commander of the ship Great Eastern, which laid the first telegraph cable connecting Europe to America. Tinakilly House's ornate staircase is reputed to be a copy of the one on this ship. Whether or not this is true is a matter of conjecture, but the Captain certainly spared no expense when he built this classical house with its fine, pitch-pine doors and shutters and ornate plasterwork ceilings. The Powers bought the house as a family home before deciding to open it as a luxurious country house hotel. They have done a splendid job, extending the home and adding rooms that fit in perfectly, furnishing the house with appropriate Victorian furniture, and adding a welcoming charm to the place. Some of the bedrooms have four-poster beds, while all twenty junior suites and two captain suites have sea views. Dining is a delight. Tinakilly is an ideal countryside base for exploring Dublin, Glendalough, and the Wicklow Mountains. *Directions:* From Dublin take the N11 (Wexford road) to Rathnew village. Turn left, towards Wicklow, and the entrance to the hotel is on your left as you leave the village.

TINAKILLY HOUSE
Owners: Josephine & Raymond Power
Rathnew, Co Wicklow, Ireland
Tel: (0404) 69274, Fax: (0404) 67806
51 Rooms, Double: €282–€702
Dinner: €60
Closed: December 24 to 26, Credit cards: all major
Ireland Blue Book
www.karenbrown.com/tinakillyhouse.html

Brian O'Hara is the sixth generation of his family to call Coopershill home since it was built in 1774. It is one of those wonderful places that offer the best of both worlds—the luxury of a country house hotel and the warmth of a home. You can even rent the entire place on a weekly basis for a house party. Brian and his wife Lindy welcome guests to their lovely home through the massive front door into the stove-warmed hall whose flagged floor is topped by an Oriental rug, and where rain gear hangs at the ready. Beyond lies a parade of lovely rooms tastefully decorated and beautifully furnished with grand, antique furniture, much of which is as old as the house itself. All but three of the bedrooms have the original four-poster or half-tester beds, but, of course, with modern mattresses. All the bedrooms are large and have private bathrooms. The only one with its bathroom down the hall requires an instruction manual to operate its magnificent shower! Ancestors' portraits gaze down upon you in the dining room, set with tables to accommodate individual parties. After an excellent dinner, guests chat round the fire over coffee. Secluded by 500 acres of farm and woodland, there are many delightful walks. Boating and fishing are available. There is enough sightseeing to justify spending a week here. *Directions:* From Dublin take the N4 to Drumfin (18 km south of Sligo). Turn right towards Riverstown and Coopershill is on your left 1 km before the village.

COOPERSHILL
Owners: Lindy & Brian O'Hara
Riverstown, Co Sligo, Ireland
Tel & Fax: (071) 91 65108
8 Rooms, Double: €230–€258
1 House: €6,000 weekly
Dinner: €55
Open: Apr to Oct, Credit cards: all major
Ireland Blue Book
www.karenbrown.com/coopershill.html

In summer, the driveway of Rosturk Woods is lined with wild red fuchsias that lead you to the low white house hugging a vast expanse of firm, sandy beach on the shores of Clew Bay. Home to Louisa and Alan Stoney and their young family (Alan grew up in the imposing castle next door, while Louisa's parents live close by), the house has the feel of an old cottage, though it is only a few years old. Bedrooms have stripped-pine doors and several have pine-paneled, sloping ceilings. There's a lot of old pine furniture, antique pieces, and attractive prints and fabrics. The house cleverly divides so that a wing of two or three large bedrooms, a living room, and a kitchen can be closed off and used as self-catering accommodation. A delightful self-catering cottage has four beds and is equipped for handicapped guests. Louisa can sometimes direct you to nearby places where traditional Irish music is played. You can play tennis on the Stoneys' court, or hire a boat for a full- or half-day trip on Clew Bay. In contrast to the lush green fields and long sandy beaches that hug Clew Bay, a short drive brings you to the wilder, more rugged scenery of Achill Island. To the south lie Newport and Westport. *Directions:* From Westport take the N59 through Newport towards Achill Island. Before you arrive in Mulrany, cross the Owengarve river and after 500 meters turn left into the woodland to Rosturk Woods.

ROSTURK WOODS
Owners: Louisa & Alan Stoney
Rosturk, Mulrany, Co Mayo, Ireland
Tel & Fax: (098) 36264
3 Rooms, Double: €100–€150
1 Cottage: €750–€1,500 weekly
Dinner: €40
Open: Feb to Nov, Credit cards: none
www.karenbrown.com/rosturk.html

Ballymaloe House is a rambling, 17th-century manor house built onto an old Norman keep surrounded by lawns, a small golf course, and 400 acres of farmland. Run by members of the extended Allen family, Ballymaloe has established a reputation for outstanding hospitality and superb food, yet everything is decidedly informal. Families are made especially welcome (play equipment, outdoor heated pool in summer, childrens' meals) and several of the rooms can be 'linked' together to accommodate them. Guests gather before dinner in the lounge to make their selections from the set menu, which offers four or five choices for each course. The bedrooms in the main house come in all shapes and sizes, from large and airy to cozy. For peace and quiet opt for one of the lovely garden rooms several of which have little patios and direct access to the garden. Surrounding a courtyard, the smaller stable bedrooms offer country-cottage charm—and beamed ceilings for those on the upper floor. Blarney and Kinsale are within easy striking distance but allow time to play a game of croquet, go for a walk or a bike ride; and explore the coast with its small rocky inlets, fishing harbors, and lonely headlands. Need a gift there's no need to go further than the car park where the Ballymaloe shop offers the best of all-things Irish. *Directions:* Ballymaloe is signposted from the N25 (Cork to Waterford road). It is 3 km beyond Cloyne on the Ballycotton road.

BALLYMALOE HOUSE
Owner: The Allen family
Manager: Hazel Allen
Shanagarry, Midleton, Co Cork, Ireland
Tel: (021) 4652531, Fax: (021) 4652021
32 Rooms, Double: €250–€320
Dinner: €65
Closed: Dec 24 to 27, Credit cards: all major
Ireland Blue Book
www.karenbrown.com/ballymaloehouse.html

The K Club began life as The Kildare Hotel & Country Club but as everyone shortened the name, they changed it. Stay here and you get preference for tee times on the championship golf courses designed by Arnold Palmer. If you do intend to play, enquire about the golf packages that include accommodation and green fees. Even if you are not a golfer, this is the most sumptuous of places to stay—the grandest of houses with a parade of luxurious, beautiful rooms. The artwork is exquisite, with a room devoted to Jack Yeats's paintings. Taking pride of place in the magnificent dining room is The Byerly Turk, a massive 17th-century portrait of one of the three stallions that sired every thoroughbred in the world. Fine cooking is an essential ingredient here and the menu includes Irish classics such as roast Wicklow lamb as well as more nirvana-like fare. Pamper yourself in the health spa, splash in the pool, or just stroll through the acres of gardens and revel in the sheer luxury of the place. Exquisite self-catering apartments are available. It is easy to understand why The K Club represents an ideal of luxury for so many people. *Directions:* Take the N7 (Kildare road) out of Dublin to Kill where you turn right for the 5-km drive to The K Club, on your left just before Straffan.

THE K CLUB
Manager: Michael Davern
Straffan, Co Kildare, Ireland
Tel: (01) 6017200, Fax: (01) 6017299
69 Rooms, Double: €495–€875
24 Apartments: €875 nightly
Dinner: €65–€75
Open: all year, Credit cards: all major
Ireland Blue Book
www.karenbrown.com/kclub.html

I arrived on a windswept stormy day to be revived by hot tea and a slice of cake. The journey was quickly forgotten as I became engrossed in Patricia's tale of training the new rooster to begin his song at 8 am, instead of dawn, to give guests a good lie in. Patricia and her husband Austin (passionate about all-things golf) are welcoming hosts, generous with their time and experts at planning trips—one along the coast and across the little ferry to Waterford is a favorite with guests. Their farmhouse dates back to 1703 and over the years various owners have made additions and changes with, most recently, Austin and Patricia's transformation. Incredibly, the soaring garden room, where you toast your toes before the fire and gather for sherry before dinner, was recently a crumbling piggery. Bedrooms come in all shapes and sizes are priced accordingly. Patricia's dinner celebrates good country food with local, organic produce. Austin offers a short, value-for-money, wine list. If you are traveling to Ireland via the Rosslare Ferry, a stay at here is an excellent introduction to Ireland or a great place to spend your last nights in the Emerald Isle. *Directions:* Tagoat is on the N25, 6 km north of Rosslare harbor. Turn between the church and pub onto R736. Churchtown House is on your left after 1 km.

CHURCHTOWN HOUSE
Owners: Patricia & Austin Cody
Tagoat, Rosslare, Co Wexford, Ireland
Tel: (053) 32555, Fax: (053) 32577
12 Rooms, Double: €110–€130
Dinner: €39 not Sun or Mon
Open: Mar 1 to Nov 1, Credit cards: all major
www.karenbrown.com/churchtown.html

Tir Na Fiúise offers you a perfect base for exploring the mid-west and Shannon region. Inez and Niall Heenan have converted the barns just down the lane from their farmhouse to self-catering accommodation rented by the week. The delightful cottages are decorated with a simple, fresh, country look. The kitchen/living areas feature solid-fuel stoves and modern appliances such as dishwashers and microwaves. The Granary is a one-bedroom cottage just perfect for a couple getting away from it all to a cozy little nook, while The Stables has two bedrooms, making it more suitable for a family or larger group. The Lime Kiln also has two bedrooms and is larger than the Stables. The area has some excellent restaurants and local pubs, which also serve great food if you don't want to cook. Inez and Niall encourage guests to explore their organic farm and adjacent bog land. You can cycle along the quiet lanes, try your hand at fishing in the nearby lough, and join in village activities. On Thursday nights, May to September, there is Irish music and dance in the village hall. If you must rush off to tourist spots, Bunratty Folk Park is an hour-and-a-half's drive away (as is Shannon airport). Closer at hand are Clonmacnois and Birr Castle. *Directions:* Nenagh is on the N7, Limerick to Dublin road. Leave the main road in Nenagh and travel through Borrisokane and Ballinderry to Terryglass. The lane leading to Tir Na Fiúise (1 km on your left) is opposite the bridge in the village.

TIR NA FIÚISE
Owners: Inez & Niall Heenan
Terryglass, Nenagh, Co Tipperary, Ireland
Tel & Fax: (067) 22041
3 Cottages: Granary €210–€310 weekly
Stables €270–€460 weekly
Lime Kiln €300–€480 weekly
Open: all year, Credit cards: MC, VS
www.karenbrown.com/tirnafiuise.html

Only in Ireland can you have a village that does not exist! Inch House is the only building in Inch while the nearest village, Bouladuff, is known and signposted only as "The Ragg" in spite of being marked as Bouladuff on maps—hence we list Inch House under Thurles! Follow the directions and you'll reach this stately Georgian home surrounded by miles of farmland. The house was built in 1720 by the Ryan family. Nora and John Egan originally came here to farm with their eight children who are now grown. Daughter Maureen works closely with her parents and chances are you'll meet one or two of the other children around the place. It's a real treat to stay here for it is quintessentially Irish and incredibly homey in spite of having ballroom-sized drawing and dining rooms resplendent with 15-foot-high ceilings. Kieran O'Dwyer is in charge of the kitchen and his set dinner menu (plenty of choices for each course) focuses on local produce. A grand sweep of polished oak stairs lead up to the bedrooms where room 26 is large enough to hold a party, room 24 has a stupendous half-tester bed, and room 27 offers a four-poster. Cashel with its famous rock is a half-hour drive away. *Directions:* From the N8 (Dublin to Cork road) take the turnoff to Thurles. Go to the town square and take the Nenagh road for 6 km past "The Ragg" and the driveway to the house is on your left.

INCH HOUSE
Owners: Nora & John Egan
Thurles, Co Tipperary, Ireland
Tel: (0504) 51348, Fax: (0504) 51754
5 Rooms, Double: €116
Dinner: €48-€50 (not Sun or Mon)
Closed: Christmas, Credit cards: MC, VS
www.karenbrown.com/inch.html

Ardtara, a grand home with well-proportioned rooms and lovely stained-glass windows, was built in 1856 by the Clark family, owners of the village linen mill. A downturn in the Clark family fortunes shut the gates for many years, and the house lay sleeping until it received a new lease on life as a country house hotel. Central heating and modern bathrooms were added, but care was taken in keeping architectural details. Many of the 16 original fireplaces have been converted to open gas fires, which give the house a cheerful warmth. All but one of the bedrooms has a cozy fireplace. It's a comfortable place where the staff, many are locals, offers a warmth welcome. Chef Olivier Boudon, also a local lad, has gained an excellent reputation for his food and takes great pride in his locally sourced produce. The impressive dining room has a hunting frieze and a ceiling dominated by an enormous glass skylight, a perfect place to enjoy Olivier's food. Just a 5 minutes drive from major roads, Ardtara is a perfect location for a day trip along the Antrim coast to visit the famous Giant's Causeway. Derry town is an hour's drive away and guests often take a guided walk around the city walls. *Directions:* From Belfast take the M2 motorway to A6 (Londonderry road). After Castledawson, take A29 towards Coleraine. Just beyond Maghera, turn right at the Upperlands and Kilrea signpost. Go through the village of Upperlands. The hotel is on your left.

ARDTARA COUNTRY HOUSE
Managers: Olivier Boudon & Valerie Ferson
8 Gorteade Road
Upperlands
Co Londonderry BT46 5SA, Northern Ireland
Tel: (028) 796 44490, Fax: (028) 796 45080
8 Rooms, Double: £150
Dinner: £28–£35
Open: all year, Credit cards: all major
www.karenbrown.com/ardtara.html

Foxmount Farms Country House is the sort of house that feels like home from the moment you walk in the front door. Margaret has been taking guests for nigh on forty years—she's a natural at hospitality and in more recent years has been joined by her husband David who loves to talk about the farm with guests and give advice on what to do and see in the area—the Waterford crystal factory is a big draw. Margaret is one of those people who shows her appreciation of her guests by feeding them lavish breakfasts. Tasty porridge cooked on the Aga with lots of cream. Scones that melt in your mouth with lashings of raspberry jam. Walk up the garden and see the fruits that she uses: strawberries, raspberries, gooseberries, apples, and rhubarb fresh from the garden. There's no shortage of places to go for dinner and you are welcome to relax and make yourself at home in the drawing room. Upstairs, the extremely comfortable bedrooms have very nice bathrooms—two with showers over the tub and two with their shower cubicles tucked into separate little closets. One has an extra bed, making it ideal for family accommodation. Just down the road is the Passage East Ferry which takes you across the river to the pretty Hook peninsula. *Directions:* Take the road from Waterford toward Dunmore East. Three km after passing the hospital, take the left fork toward Passage East. Foxmount Farms is signposted on the right after 500 meters.

FOXMOUNT FARMS COUNTRY HOUSE
Owners: Margaret & David Kent
Passage East Road
Waterford, Co Waterford, Ireland
Tel: (051) 874308, Fax: (051) 854906
5 Rooms, Double: €110
Open: Mar to Oct, Credit cards: none
www.karenbrown.com/foxmountfarm.html

The owner's plans for Clonard House, begun in 1783, showed a grand three-story structure. Skirmishes with the British continually interrupted construction, so he got no further than the second floor, leaving the grand central staircase to curve into the ceiling. A working farm with all the machinery in back, the massive front door opens to a smile and a traditional Irish welcome from Kathleen Hayes who takes a great interest in her guests and pride in her home. I particularly enjoyed Kathleen's high-ceilinged sitting room with its peach-colored walls and chairs covered in soft colors coordinating with draperies and carpet. Crisp white cloth covers the little tables in the attractive breakfast room. For dinner, guests often go to restaurants in nearby fishing villages. Bedrooms are not grand country-house affairs—by and large they are snug in size. Several years ago Kathleen had a yen for four-poster beds so several rooms sport them All have TVs, en suite showers, and hairdryers. Being just a short drive from Rosslare, Clonard House is ideal for your first or last nights in Ireland if you are arriving by ferry. Sightseeing attractions nearby include the Irish National Heritage Park, Wexford, and Johnstown Castle. *Directions:* From Rosslare travel 13 km towards Wexford, make a left at the first roundabout (N25), left at the second roundabout onto the R733, and immediately left to Clonard House.

CLONARD HOUSE
Owners: Kathleen & John Hayes
Wexford, Clonard Great
Co Wexford, Ireland
Tel & Fax: (053) 43141
9 Rooms, Double: €100
Open: Mar to mid-Nov, Credit cards: MC, VS
www.karenbrown.com/clonard.html

Youghal (pronounced "you all" with an American southern drawl), a workaday fishing port, is beginning to flaunt its historic past: drab, gray buildings are being restored, empty shopfronts are coming to life. Standing amongst them, Aherne's old-world pub exterior is decked out in shiny new paint. Owned by the Fitzgibbon family since 1923, Aherne's includes a seafood restaurant and bedrooms. There's an old-world, traditional atmosphere in the bars where you can enjoy a pint with the locals and an array of tempting bar food. The restaurant specializes in locally caught seafood and the menu changes daily, depending on what is fresh and available. In the guests' sitting room, a cozy fire is flanked by comfortable sofas and a coffee table stacked with books on all-things Irish. Three ground-floor bedrooms offer easy access, with one specially equipped for wheelchairs. I particularly enjoyed the upstairs rooms, which have little balconies facing the courtyard. If you want privacy, request one of the suites in the adjacent townhouse. All guestrooms have attractive decor, antique furniture, and large firm beds, each accompanied by an immaculate bathroom. For a stay of longer than a couple of nights the Fitzgibbons have a luxurious, two-bedroom penthouse apartment with breathtaking views of the harbor. *Directions:* Youghal is between Waterford and Cork on the N25. Aherne's is on the main street in town.

AHERNE'S
Owners: Gaye, Kate, John & David Fitzgibbon
163 North Main Street
Youghal, Co Cork, Ireland
Tel: (024) 92424, Fax: (024) 93633
13 Rooms, Double: €160–€230
1 Apartment: €450–€800 weekly
Dinner: €48
Closed: Christmas, Credit cards: all major
Ireland Blue Book
www.karenbrown.com/ahernes.html

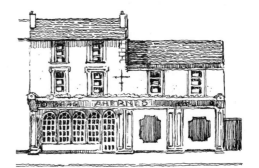

Index

Index

Index

BROWN wrote her first travel guide in 1976. Her personalized travel series has grown to 17 titles, which Karen and her small staff work diligently to keep updated. Karen, her husband, Rick, and their children, Alexandra and Richard, live in Moss Beach, a small town on the coast south of San Francisco. They settled here in 1991 when they opened Seal Cove Inn. Karen is frequently traveling but when she is home, in her role as innkeeper, enjoys welcoming Karen Brown readers.

JUNE EVELEIGH BROWN'S love of travel was inspired by the *National Geographic* magazines that she read as a girl in her dentist's office—so far she has visited over 40 countries. June hails from Sheffield, England and lived in Zambia and Canada before moving to northern California where she lives in San Mateo with her husband, Tony, their daughter Clare, their two German Shepherds, and a Siamese cat.

BARBARA MACLURCAN TAPP, the talented artist who produces all of the hotel sketches and delightful illustrations in this guide, was raised in Sydney, Australia where she studied interior design. Although Barbara continues with architectural rendering and watercolor painting, she devotes much of her time to illustrating the Karen Brown guides. Barbara lives in Kensington, California, with her husband, Richard, and is Mum to Jono, Alex and Georgia.

JANN POLLARD, The artist of the cover painting has studied art since childhood, and is well known for her outstanding impressionistic-style watercolors. Jann's original paintings are represented through The Gallery in Burlingame, CA and New Masters Gallery in Carmel, CA. *www.jannpollard.com.* Fine art giclée prints of her paintings are available at www.karenbrown.com.

Watch for a New Thriller Series
Featuring "Karen Brown"
As Travel Writer & Undercover Sleuth

Author M. Diane Vogt, the creator of the critically acclaimed and popular Judge Wilhelmina Carson legal suspense novels, is writing a new series featuring the exploits of "Karen Brown".

Combine the heroic salvage consultant Travis McGee – from John D. MacDonald's hugely successful Ft. Lauderdale mystery/thriller series with *Under the Tuscan Sun's* Frances Mayes, and that's Karen Brown, clandestine recovery specialist and world renowned travel writer.

Based on actual places and destinations as featured in Karen Brown's guides, join Karen in her travels as by day she inspects charming hotels, and by night she dabbles in intrigue and defeats the world of killers, scoundrels, and scam artists.

The series has been launched with the publication of James Patterson's best selling book, *Thriller*. The short story, "Surviving Toronto" introduces sleuth, Karen Brown.

Awards coming soon......

Quality

Reader feedback will be used to evaluate and award exceptional quality and service for Karen Brown Recommended Properties.

On our website Karen Brown Travelers will have the ability to vote for a property in a number of categories, including but not limited to; best breakfast, location/setting, welcome, comfort/ambiance, value, and romance.

Service

Ambiance

Karen Brown Presents Her Own Special Hideaways

Karen Brown's Seal Cove Inn

Spectacularly set amongst wildflowers and bordered by cypress trees, Seal Cove Inn (Karen's second home) looks out to the distant ocean. Each room has a fireplace, cozy sitting area, and a view of the sea. Located on the coast, 35 minutes south of San Francisco.

Seal Cove Inn, Moss Beach, California
toll free telephone: (800) 995-9987
www.sealcoveinn.com

Karen Brown's Dolphin Cove Inn

Hugging a steep hillside overlooking the sparkling deep-blue bay of Manzanillo, Dolphin Cove Inn offers guests outstanding value. Each room has either a terrace or a balcony, and a breathtaking view of the sea. Located on the Pacific Coast of Mexico.

Dolphin Cove Inn, Manzanillo, Mexico
toll free telephone: (866) 360-9062
www.dolphincoveinn.com